INTRODUCTION TO
FOREIGN
EXCHANGE

INTRODUCTION TO
FOREIGN EXCHANGE

RUDI WEISWEILLER

SECOND EDITION

WOODHEAD-FAULKNER

Published by Woodhead-Faulkner Ltd
Fitzwilliam House, 32 Trumpington Street, Cambridge CB2 1QY
and
51 Washington Street, Dover, NH 03820, USA

First published 1983
Second edition 1984

© Rudi Weisweiller 1983, 1984

ISBN 0 85941 286 5 (Paper)
ISBN 0 85941 285 7 (Cased)

Library of Congress Cataloging in Publication Data
Weisweiller Rudi
Introduction to Foreign Exchange
Revised edition of Foreign Exchange 1972
Includes index
1. Foreign exchange
I Weisweiller, Rudi Foreign Exchange
II Title
HG3821.W44 1984 332.4 5 84 50644
ISBN 0 85941 285 7
ISBN 0 85941 286 5 (PB)

Conditions of sale
All rights reserved. No part of this publication may be
reproduced, stored in a retrieval system or transmitted, in any
form or by any means, electronic, mechanical, photocopying,
recording or otherwise, without the prior permission of the
copyright holder.

Design by Geoff Green

Typesetting by Hands Fotoset, Leicester
Printed in Great Britain by
St Edmundsbury Press, Bury St Edmunds
Suffolk

PREFACE
TO THE SECOND EDITION

The first edition of this book met with considerable response and seems to have satisfied a need among those for whom it was written. The undiminished concern about currency problems suggests that this simple exposition of complex issues will continue to be widely appreciated.

The changes made to this edition are twofold. I have added sections about sovereign risks (Chapter 14) and about currency options (Chapter 3), the two topics which have received wider notice in 1983 than ever before. I have also tried to make the book even easier to read by placing the chapters in a different sequence, by rewording certain sections (in particular, in Chapters 2, 3 and 16) and by redesigning the graph on page 9. I would like to thank The Institute of Bankers for their constructive comments on the first edition of this book.

RUDI WEISWEILLER

PREFACE
TO THE FIRST EDITION

This book is intended for the sophisticated businessman, the manager in industry or banking, the student of economics, the politician or civil servant concerned with international finance, as a systematic introduction to the complex field of foreign exchange.

It does not claim to deal with problems which concern only the full-time professional in the foreign exchange market; its aim is to ease the first steps towards a fuller understanding of the situations which arise because different countries use different currencies.

Messrs George Allen & Unwin of London kindly agreed to my using in changed or unchanged form some parts of my book *Foreign Exchange,* which they published in 1972. That book was also published by Prugg Verlag of Vienna in 1978 as *Devisen: Werkzeug des Welthandels.* Some of the new sections in the German edition were later translated into English by Adrian Weisweiller.

The contents of this book differ substantially from what I wrote a decade ago. The purpose of the book, however, is the same.

RUDI WEISWEILLER

CONTENTS

	Page
Preface to the second edition	v
Preface to the first edition	vii

1 Why foreign exchange?   1
    Basic principles   1
    Whom the market serves   5

2 How the market works   8
    Foreign exchange dealing systems   8
    Dealing between centres   14
    The problem of language   16
    Some foreign exchange terms   17
    A united market   20

3 Six choices   22
    Choice 1: Spot or forward?   22
    Choice 2: Time options or swaps?   26
    Choice 3: Invoicing in one's own currency or in foreign currency?   27
    Choice 4: Do banks advise or merely serve?   30
    Choice 5: Loyalty or selection?   32
    Choice 6: Financial futures: hedging or gambling?   34
    Choice 7: Currency options: an essential tool in certain situations   35

4 Money across frontiers   37
    The theory of interest arbitrage   37
    Covered arbitrage   38
    Practice versus theory   40

		Page
	Hot money	41
	The meaning and significance of forward rates	43
	Interest arbitrage and business transactions	44
5	Bretton Woods and after	48
	Intervention points	49
	Intervention in the forward market	50
	Intervention in the spot market	51
	The philosophy and its effects	52
	The change to floating	53
	Crawling pegs	54
	Monetary reform	55
	Basket currencies	56
6	The sterling area	58
	A currency area	59
	An exchange control area	59
7	The European currency	62
	The Werner Plan	62
	The snake	64
	The European Monetary System	66
	Advantages and disadvantages	66
8	Gold	69
	The history of gold	69
	Different uses	70
	Gold crises	71
	Demonetization in theory	72
	Demonetization in practice	72
	Gold or paper money	74
	Prospects	75
9	Liquidity, reserves and Special Drawing Rights	77
	What reserves are for	77
	How Special Drawing Rights are used	79

		Page
	The future of world liquidity	80
	Special Drawing Rights as numeraire	81
	Special Drawing Rights as a world currency	81
10	Currency freedom	84
	Convertibility	84
	Why exchange control?	85
	The future of exchange control	87
11	Capital movements	91
	Special rates for money flows	91
	The pros and cons	91
	Lessons to be learned from the United Kingdom's investment currency	93
12	For or against speculators	96
	Who are the 'speculators'?	96
	Role of the speculator	98
	Governments versus speculation	101
13	The causes of currency crises and their cure	103
	To tell or not to tell	103
	Causes of currency crises	104
	Difficulties of avoidance	107
	Disadvantages of persistent surplus	109
	Steps to be taken	111
	Controls and restrictions	114
	Prevention of currency crises	114
14	Eurodollars	117
	Origins of the Eurodollar	118
	Uses of the Eurodollar	119
	Development of the Eurodollar market	121
	The future	123
	Dangers	125
	Risks to industry	127
15	Forecasting exchange rates	130

		Page
	Why?	130
	How?	130
	When?	132
16	Charting a course through turbulent seas	134
	Inflation rates as indicators	135
	The effect of interest rates on exchange rates	135
	Trade figures and money flows as major influences	137
	Politics and fashion in a free market	138
	Further reading	140
	Index	142

1
WHY FOREIGN EXCHANGE?

When one goes into a shop and buys something which was made abroad, whether it is a Swiss watch, some French wine, a German motor car or a Dutch cheese, one causes a *foreign exchange deal* to take place.

Let us use Scotch whisky drunk in the United States as our example. There are two ways in which the businessman who sells it in the USA can pay the distiller of the whisky who lives in Scotland. The first way is to send US dollars to Scotland. The supplier, however, cannot normally spend these in his own country and therefore would have to exchange them for British pounds; he has to ask a bank to change the dollars into pounds. In this case, the Scottish supplier and his banker do a foreign exchange transaction together, each taking one kind of national money and giving the other.

There is another way of paying. Knowing that US dollars are not legal tender in Scotland and that, when received from the American buyer in payment for whisky, they have to be exchanged by him at his bank, the Scottish supplier may decide to avoid this effort with its attendant delays and expenses: he may ask the American businessman to pay in British pounds; in other words, he invoices the whisky to the buyer in British currency. If this is the case, it is the buyer who has to go to his bank in the United States, change some US dollars into British pounds and then send these to Scotland. The foreign exchange deal has been done between the buyer and his bank in the United States.

Basic principles

Whether the foreign exchange deal is done in the United

States or Great Britain does not affect the fundamental nature of the transaction. Indeed, certain basic conclusions about foreign exchange can be drawn from this or any similar example.

First, if a business transaction involving money has been concluded between residents of different currency areas, it necessarily involves a foreign exchange deal. This simple statement explains the existence of foreign exchange markets with their expensive machinery and highly paid dealers. It explains the unavoidable preoccupation of those concerned with economic problems, whether academics or politicians, with the international section of economic activity and its barometer, *the balance of payments*. It shows that international trade leads inevitably to foreign exchange, and that foreign exchange leads frequently to problems for nations, companies and individuals. (It also explains why this book was written.)

Second, a foreign exchange deal is merely an exchanging of one currency or national money for another. It is like any other business deal in that one thing is exchanged for another, but it differs in that, whereas usually we exchange goods for money or money for goods, in foreign exchange money is exchanged for money.

This last remark leads us inevitably to a further point which is not without significance. If the relationship between goods and money in ordinary business transactions is expressed by the price, then this is equally true in foreign exchange: the *exchange rate* is the price of the one currency expressed in terms of the other. It expresses a price relationship.

There is, however, a difference in practice between exchange rates and ordinary prices which is all too rarely recognized and heeded. When an ordinary price moves up or down, one is usually entitled to seek the reason in a change in the demand for, or the supply of, the goods. For example, when peas get more expensive, this tends to be due to a shortage of supply for seasonal or special reasons, or to an increase in demand because of a change in fashion or because alternative foodstuffs have disappeared or become more expensive. One does not ascribe the change in the price of ordinary goods to a lessening in the value of money, unless one is either studying a large number of price increases which appear to coincide and also to lack separate explanations connected with demand and supply, or comparing prices over a period of years or even decades. Only in such circumstances does it make sense to say that fares have gone up from the equivalent of 20p to 60p in 15 years, not because transport is harder to organize or more costly to provide, but because money has been greatly reduced in value. It is still necessary to decide to what extent the change in fares is due to the reduction in the purchasing power of the currency, and to what extent a change in the demand–supply situation has altered the real price of the service.

The foreign exchange rate is different, even in the short run. It expresses a relationship between two national monies. It is therefore unrealistic to assume that changes, even over the shortest period, express alterations in the demand for, or supply of, only one of these national monies. Whenever an exchange rate moves, this can be due to a change in the value of one or the other currency, or partly of one and partly of the other.

It is very tempting to see changes in rates of exchange as reflecting necessarily some alteration in the demand for, and supply of, our own currency, and very wrong to rejoice when our own currency appreciates or to plunge into the depths of gloom when its price drops. How often do we in fact look, as we should, at the economy of the country with whose currency we are comparing our own currency in the exchange rate under review? It could be that events in that country explain some or all of the change, and that our own currency has not really caused the change in rate. Comparison of the performance of both currencies with a third currency can ususally throw useful light on the reasons for a movement in exchange rates, although these can be obscured by a variety of incidental factors which may be hard to isolate or analyse.

The danger of looking only at one of the two currencies covered by the currency comparison is well illustrated by a

Press report seen some time ago. 'Some of the selling of sterling in the morning', the newspaper said, 'was against dollars but some was against French francs, which consequently turned stronger in the afternoon.' Foreign exchange language is often a deliberate attempt to make things sound more complicated than they really are. 'Stronger' and 'firmer' are standard ways of saying 'more expensive'. Therefore, all this report said was that some people were selling pounds against dollars and some were selling pounds against French francs. The French francs 'consequently turned stronger in the afternoon'; in other words, they got more expensive. Why? Because if you sell pounds and buy dollars, you are increasing the demand for dollars. As some of the selling was against French francs, they were looking for French francs and bidding up the price. Pounds were getting weaker against dollars and against French francs. This report, which sounds so obscure, 'some of the selling was against dollars and some was against French francs, which consequently turned stronger in the afternoon', is really stating the obvious: if you sell pounds against French francs, French francs must get more expensive.

The obscurity of the report is increased by the suggestion that pounds got cheaper against French francs in the morning and that French francs became more expensive against pounds in the afternoon. This is absurd as the two statements are, in fact, identical and must not give the appearance of a causal relationship. These two price changes must of course have taken place simultaneously.

Third, foreign exchange deals depend upon international commercial transactions for their existence. Unless people in one currency area buy from people in another currency area (and vice versa, for otherwise the balance of payments of the first area would be in an awful mess), there is no need for foreign exchange deals.

Every foreign exchange transaction carried out anywhere in the world is a link in a chain at the ends of which there are two customers who wish to exchange foreign currencies in opposite directions. It does not matter how many links are in a particular chain; the efficiency of the market is helped by the length of the chain, the multiplicity of professional middlemen or banks. It does, however, matter that at both ends of each chain stand people who are exchanging one currency for another because they themselves have done business with someone abroad. Thus, every exchange deal between two banks in sterling against dollars presupposes an American buying British goods, services, land or investments, and a resident of the United Kingdom buying American goods, services, land or investments. If one of the currencies is bought by someone in a third country, this establishes no exception to the rule, as he in turn only wishes to hold such currency insofar as he or somebody else can eventually buy goods, services, land or investments in the country whose currency he has bought.

Whom the market serves

The mention of goods, services, land and investments brings us to a further analysis of the elementary uses of the foreign exchange market. There are four groups of reasons which bring people into the foreign exchange market as buyers or sellers of foreign currencies.

The first group of reasons is covered by the previous reference to goods, services, land and investments. It can be covered by the term 'commercial reasons' and includes such transactions as foreign travel, the purchase of foreign stocks and shares, the sale of a factory to a company in another currency area, commissions or royalties received from abroad, as well as ordinary payments for imports and receipts from exports.

The second group is closely tied to the short-term investment of spare funds in the money markets. Investors of such funds sometimes seek higher returns abroad without regard to the risks of a possible change in exchange rates; these investments are then loosely termed 'hot money' and need to be included in the third category which is described in the next paragraph. More often, however, these funds are moved across frontiers and into another currency only when the exchange risk can be eliminated by a contract for future delivery at the same time as the initial deal is made for immediate delivery. The theory describing the rules for this considerable volume of transactions is known as *interest arbitrage* and is described in more detail in Chapter 4.

The third reason for entering the foreign exchange market is 'speculation': the desire to buy what one does not need, but hopes later to sell at a profit to those who do; or the desire to sell for future delivery what one does not have or expect to have, but hopes to buy at a lower price before one has to deliver it. Essentially, to buy a house for oneself to live in at an opportune time and in a place which one deems likely to become more popular is a good investment; to buy a house at the same time and in the same place merely to enable one to sell at a profit and not to live in is speculation.

Chapter 12 deals in more detail with the concept of speculation and some of the strong opinions people hold about it. There is no doubt, however, that some professional dealers, many of them banks all over the world, have no choice but to be long or short of currencies in pursuit of the service they give their commercial customers. They would, of course, try to do so without losing money. Their activity is covered by neither of the first two categories, although it is often carried out in conjunction with deals within them.

The fourth and last category, however closely tied to the activities of traders, investors and money men, cannot be regarded as coming legitimately within the three groups already described. At a later stage, the international monetary system set up at Bretton Woods in 1944 and enshrined in the rules of the International Monetary Fund will be discussed. Here it suffices to note that the central banks of all countries which belong to the International Monetary Fund were not only obliged to deal at the so-called 'intervention points' for spot delivery until the changes in the statutes which followed the widespread adoption of floating exchange rates in the seventies, but are in addition allowed to enter the spot or forward market at any level. Such voluntary intervention by a central bank is usually motivated by one of six reasons.

1. The central bank may be fact-finding, trying by its

own action to measure the force of market trends.
2. The central bank may be intent on building up its own currency reserves or those of another country, or on reducing them.
3. The central bank may wish to prove that it will resist an attack on its own currency with all the reserve resources at its disposal.
4. The central bank may wish at times of crisis to give the impression, without being seen to do so, that its own currency is more generally wanted than it really is.
5. The central bank may want to keep the exchange rate at a particular level in spite of market trends which, if unchecked, would move it elsewhere.
6. The central bank may wish to reduce violent fluctuations in exchange rates, the so-called peaks and troughs, which arise from a build-up of demand or supply due to seasonal, monetary or political factors and which in a period of floating rates can cause temporary rate changes of alarming magnitude.

Whether a central bank intervenes in its own name, through another central bank or through the kind offices of a commercial bank at home or abroad will depend largely on which of the six reasons predominates at that moment. The detection by commentators of massive intervention is important to those in the market, whether bankers or their customers, and the method used by the central bank must be chosen with this fact in mind. Central banks have gained much experience of market intervention in the years since the Bretton Woods system became generally operational after the post-war re-opening of the London Foreign Exchange Market in December 1951. They proceed with great skill and usually manage to serve the interests of government without destroying the viability and freedom of the foreign exchange market.

2
HOW THE MARKET WORKS

As established in Chapter 1, foreign exchange dealing is the result of international business of one kind or another. Deals only take place when people do business with someone in another country. They need to exchange one national currency for another, and this exchange is accomplished with the intervention of one or several banks. Obviously, if a number of such transactions takes place, a market is the right term for the organizational structure which results.

Foreign exchange dealing systems

The *foreign exchange market* differs from most markets in that it is truly and inevitably international. Foreign exchange deals do not become necessary unless people in different currency areas do business with each other. Indeed, in every foreign exchange deal businessmen in two countries must be involved (see Figure 2.1).

The idea of a national foreign exchange market is, therefore, in one sense inappropriate. At best, the local market is part of an international organization, a national centre for a truly international activity.

In practice, as in most fields of commercial activity, those who need to exchange one currency for another rarely meet without the intervention of an intermediary. The world over, the chief intermediaries for this type of business are banks: they act as principals on their own account and seek to find another bank at home or abroad with the opposite deal in mind. It is the object of this chapter to explain how they do this.

The commercial transactions

Transaction 1

Citizen A in Country A buys potatoes from Citizen B in Country B.

Citizen B in Country B sells potatoes to Citizen A in Country A.

Transaction 2

Citizen Alpha in Country A sells peanuts to Citizen Beta in Country B.

Citizen Beta in Country B buys peanuts from Citizen Alpha in Country A.

The foreign exchange deals

In respect of transaction 1

Either – Citizen A sends Currency A to Citizen B, which Citizen B then sells to a bank to obtain Currency B. Or – Citizen A buys Currency B with his own Currency A and then sends this Currency B to Citizen B. (In either event, Currency A is sold to a bank and Currency B is thereby bought.)

In respect of transaction 2

Either – Citizen Alpha receives Currency A, which Citizen Beta has bought from a bank with his own Currency B. Or – Citizen Alpha receives Currency B from Citizen Beta and sells it to a bank to obtain Currency A. (In either event, Currency A is bought from a bank and Currency B is thereby sold.)

The result

With the help of banks (the Foreign Exchange market) two foreign exchange deals (which resulted from the two commercial deals) have been carried out. They are in opposite directions. If they are also equal in size, the balance of trade is in equilibrium and the currency reserves of countries A and B neither gain nor lose.

Figure 2.1. The role of the foreign exchange deal.

Foreign exchange brokers

Within the larger of the world's foreign exchange centres, the number of banks operating foreign exchange departments is such as to require a highly developed and efficient system of foreign exchange brokers to act as go-betweens in the foreign exchange deals which any of the banks may wish to enter into with any of their neighbours. Although less than half the banks maintain active dealing rooms, this, nevertheless, makes for markets of a size and versatility in which only a measure of specialization and a high degree of organization can avoid chaos and frustration.

The rules of the market are simple. The foreign exchange brokers are somewhat like brokers on a stock exchange, but they do not act as principals. They inform and introduce; when business between two banks results, they confirm the arrangement and collect a brokerage.

In recent years many firms of foreign exchange brokers have either established branches in other centres or entered into long-term affiliations with existing firms abroad. This enables them to act as links between banks in different countries and even continents, thus making the concept of a worldwide market both easier to achieve in practice and less costly in terms of rapid communication than was possible when banks relied entirely on direct dealing for their currency deals with banks overseas.

When the London Foreign Exchange Market re-opened in December 1951, the pre-war number of firms operating as foreign exchange brokers had been reduced, mainly through mergers, to eight. Only a few more were added as the market grew in the three decades which followed. These firms each cover a number of major currencies; each major currency is covered by several brokers, giving banks a reasonable measure of choice in selecting a broker but without so diluting the market as to make individual brokers ill-informed and ineffective.

The basic function performed by foreign exchange brokers is to tell banks the rate at which there are firm buyers and firm sellers available in the market at any time.

They will give this information in reply to a specific enquiry from a particular bank about a pair of currencies to be exchanged, for spot delivery or for a stated forward date. They will also offer this information unasked to some or all the banks with whom they are in regular contact, whenever a change in the rate or some other event makes them feel that such information may be of use to the dealers in the banks.

When a foreign exchange dealer in a bank wishes to buy or sell foreign currency he can tell one of the brokers specializing in that currency and give him an order to buy or sell, which will be for a stated amount at a price stated or within a stated limit, and which will be valid until explicitly withdrawn or until a stated time. The broker immediately informs all banks with whom he is in regular contact – and to whose dealing rooms he has usually one or several direct telephone lines – of the proposition made. At this stage he does not give the name of the originator or any hint of his identity, although exceptions are sometimes allowed when the originator is, at one extreme, a central bank or, at the other extreme, a small bank wishing to deal in an exceptionally large amount or for delivery a long time ahead.

The broker will receive varying reactions to his proposal and with those whose response shows some interest he will talk further. After checking the whole market and perhaps negotiating with a few banks he may revert to the originator with a firm counter-proposal. If two banks eventually agree to deal, the broker will tell each the name of the other. A confirmation and a bill for brokerage will be sent to both of them by the broker, who may tell all the other banks on his circuit that business was done and at what price. He will still not tell them the names of the two banks involved.

It is one of the main activities of brokers to tell the banks at what rates business has recently been transacted or is now proposed. The system assures banks of the speedy and anonymous passing of information to all members of the market, and this is the chief advantage of the brokers' system. Considering the small amount of time and effort which banks have to contribute to the achievement of individual deals, the brokerage charged does not seem excessive.

There is another way in which banks can and do use the brokers and which, provided the brokers are fully in the picture all the time (which is feasible and probable when a large proportion of the total business passes through the brokers), is of value. Dealers ask the brokers for information even when they have no immediate proposition to make. While brokers obviously hope for some orders, and indeed some orders with a prospect of actual brokerage-earning business, they will also readily tell dealers what is going on elsewhere in the market. The dealer who has enquiries from industrial customers or from abroad relies heavily on such information long before he has himself done a deal and thus is in a position to give an order to a broker in cover thereof. This function of the brokers' market as a source of accurate and up-to-the-minute information is a very important aspect of the system.

Brokers' markets exist in many centres. Those in London, New York, Amsterdam and Paris are the most highly developed.

Deposit brokers

The development of the Eurocurrency markets, described in greater detail in Chapter 14, has brought a new activity to the dealing rooms of most banks and one which has grown rapidly since its inception in the late fifties.

Banks borrow from and lend to industrial firms of various sizes, commercial and central banks, state agencies and international organizations large amounts of currencies other than their own.

This business is really more appropriate to the cashier's department or the credit officers of the bank than to the foreign exchange traders. Nevertheless, it has become customary to leave foreign exchange dealers to handle it because they tend to have the necessary knowledge of the overseas banking and commercial scene, are in frequent contact with likely partners abroad and often speak several foreign languages.

In these activities foreign exchange dealers have increasingly utilized the services of foreign currency deposit brokers to find them suitable counterparties in their own centre or elsewhere, to check credit-standing and limit-availability and to fix up business. Where loans result, both parties pay a fixed brokerage.

Many of the foreign exchange deposit brokers are firms which also operate as ordinary foreign exchange brokers, but usually different teams working in separate rooms attend to these two activities. Close contact is necessary as foreign exchange swaps frequently connect a borrowing activity in one currency and a lending activity in another. The essential difference between buying and selling and borrowing and lending is, however, not forgotten.

The daily meeting

Many European countries have a foreign exchange market which, for part of each day, has, unlike the telephonic markets in London, New York or Hong Kong, a physical meeting-place, generally in a special room within the building of the local stock exchange. This physical foreign exchange market is not customary in English-speaking countries and therefore has no name in the English language. Dealers refer to it as the *foreign exchange bourse* or the *fixing*.

Those who are used to operating on a foreign exchange bourse find this system quick and efficient. Others regard it as merely time-wasting and noisy; it certainly makes anonymity impossible by forcing dealers to make their bids and offers in public. Until the International Foreign Exchange Club was founded (through the initiative of a Frenchman, Maurice Plaquet) in the late fifties, the international and local gatherings of which bring dealers together for informal professional discussion, daily bourse meetings certainly established personal contact between local dealers in a way which was then sadly lacking in London and New York.

The bourse operates much like a stock exchange or commodity market. Like these it has one great advantage: the final price of the day, based on the business actually brought into the market, is made public immediately. Not only can it be used as a basis for legal agreements, but in many countries it also forms the basis for the exchange rates used between banks and their customers. No such norm exists in the United Kingdom or the United States and the fixing of the exchange rate, therefore, leaves room for doubt, negotiation and argument. This may in practice turn out to be to the advantage of the customer; many continental banks prefer the official fixing, which is the natural result of the daily meeting at the bourse.

Direct dealing

The other method used for foreign exchange dealing between banks in the same centre is for the dealers of one bank to get in touch by telephone or by telex with the dealers of another bank. Once upon a time this system was the only one used in Switzerland and was workable because there were in that country relatively few, although large and active, foreign exchange dealing rooms. It seems cumbersome for banks to operate without the aid of either brokers or a physical meeting-place, but some foreign exchange dealers are accustomed to this system and prefer it. Recently, United Kingdom banks too have been authorized to deal direct on the telephone or the telex with each other, but they still tend to transact much of their foreign exchange business through brokers.

Most other European foreign exchange markets use a combination of the three systems: the daily meeting, direct dealing and brokers. They meet once a day at the central exchange, but before and after the daily meeting, while in their respective offices, they get in touch with each other by telephone or telex. In most countries there are also brokers who can intervene between the local banks much as the London brokers do and who can supplement the direct-dealing method. As, however, they have no exclusive right to the business being negotiated between the local banks they tend to be offered a rather large proportion of proposals which are difficult or impossible to turn into brokerage-earning deals. In some countries the foreign exchange brokers are compensated for this disadvantage by having some official function at the daily fixing for which handsome commissions are paid.

Dealing between centres

So far our attention has been focused mainly on the different ways in which banks in a financial centre communicate with each other, convey or obtain information, and negotiate foreign exchange deals between members of the same market, thus ensuring that, apart from minor variations, the same price will be asked and offered for the same currency by all banks in the same country at any one time. We must now turn our attention to international deals, which are after all the fundamental ones in terms of the service rendered by the foreign exchange markets to those taking part in international trade and investment.

A large proportion of the foreign exchange deals done each day is between banks in different countries. These deals are often the direct consequence of the wishes of the banks' customers to buy or sell currencies needed to pay for goods or services or received in payment of goods or services. Others are between the banks only and do not have an immediate commercial transaction underlying them; they serve to even out temporary differences in the level of demand and supply in various centres and to make sure that at any one time the rate for a certain currency is the same not only everywhere in one country, but everywhere in the world. It is necessary to add that 'the world' to the foreign exchange man means those parts of it which are awake and working at that time of day.

When banks wish to be in touch with others with whom they maintain a regular business relationship to discuss foreign exchange matters, to seek or give information, to make bids or offers for currencies and to negotiate deals, or to borrow or lend currencies, their dealers will approach them by telephone, telex or cable. The method chosen will depend on technical circumstances like cost, the degree of urgency or the availability of lines and machines, as also on the inclination of the dealers involved, coloured by the particular purpose of the call and the type of discussion expected. Where poor connections or linguisitic difficulties are feared, the telex will be preferred to the telephone. Where hard bargaining is expected, persuasion needed or general information being sought, the telephone will usually be more satisfactory than the telex.

The problem of language [1]

As so much of the foreign exchange dealer's life is lived on the telephone and telex, and most of it on calls where distances are great and costs therefore high, it is only natural that a distinct language should have developed between the world's relatively few foreign exchange professionals. Time is money for the foreign exchange dealer in an even more direct sense than for everybody else.

The foreign exchange vocabulary consists of two kinds of words: those which are the proper technical terms of the trade and, far more numerous, those which have developed and are used in conversations between the professionals, the dealers and the brokers. The words in this second group should not be used when explaining foreign exchange matters to customers, to non-foreign-exchange people in the banks or to journalists. They are used all too often

---

[1] Glossaries of foreign exchange terms can be found in:
A Dictionary of International Finance, J. Walmsley (Macmillan 1979);
Foreign Exchange Today (revised edition), Raymond G. F. Coninx (Woodhead-Faulkner 1980);
Foreign Exchange Management, T. W. McRae & D. P. Walker (Prentice Hall 1980);
Foreign Exchange Risk, A. R. Prindl (John Wiley 1976);
Foreign Exchange and the Corporate Treasurer, J. Heywood (A. & C. Black 1978).

outside the market and cause obscurity. This leads to a failure in communication. The consequences of this include a widespread belief in the obscurity of all topics related to foreign exchange and sometimes an inability on the part of customers to obtain urgently needed help and advice in this field of banking. Dealers ought to be aware of the importance of lucid explanation in terms intelligible to the layman when talking about foreign exchange matters to those outside the market, and of the unfortunate results, upon their own careers as well as upon the business of their customers, if they fail to translate their expert knowledge into the native idiom.

Some foreign exchange terms

There are several unavoidable foreign exchange terms with which even the non-expert must be familiar if his work involves him in serious confrontation with the subject, whether for political or commercial reasons. Six of these terms are dealt with here, namely spot and forward, premium and discount, cross rates and swaps.

Spot and forward

All foreign exchange contracts entered into by two parties, whether they are bankers or not, are legally binding whether oral or written and are for a specific value date. On this date, delivery of one currency will be made by A to B and of the other currency by B to A. The value date is also called the delivery date. It is important, and sometimes frankly irritating, that delivery of both currencies must be made on the same day and that, because of this, contracts can only be made for a date which is a 'good date' or working day in the countries of both currencies. For example, Good Friday is not usually a holiday in New York, but it is impossible to buy US dollars for delivery on Good Friday with pounds, because there is a holiday in the United Kingdom and therefore one of the currencies cannot be delivered.

This problem apart, currency deals can be agreed for any working day that suits both parties to the contract. It can be as far in the future as desired, although few contracts are for periods over 1 year and, even in the most important currencies, deals are rare for delivery dates beyond 5 years. Deals are known as *forward deals* unless they are for delivery within the next few days, in which case they are called *spot deals*. Here it is necessary to differentiate between 'spot' as meaning any delivery within the next few days and 'spot' (as more usually understood) as meaning delivery 2 working days from today. This latter and better-known interpretation of 'spot' should really be called *ordinary spot*.

Premium and discount

The price of any currency for different delivery dates tends to vary even at the same moment. In Chapters 3 and 4 we will discuss both why this is so and some of the reasons which might influence buyers or sellers to cover for a delivery date even at prices which look unattractive. Here we are concerned with the fact of these differences, not with the whys and wherefores. When foreign currencies for different dates are being traded at different prices, these differences are expressed with reference to the price for ordinary spot (2-day delivery). If the currency in question is more expensive for forward delivery than for ordinary spot, it is said to be *at a premium*. If it is cheaper, it is said to be *at a discount*.

Because it is customary to quote foreign currency in the United Kingdom not in terms of the sterling price per one unit of foreign currency but in terms of how many units of foreign currency can be bought with one pound, the following calculations result for those who see exchange rates from a British point of view.

Spot US dollars against sterling: $1.90 per £ ($1.9000)
3 months' forward: $1.89½ per £ ($1.8950)
i.e. dollars are at a premium of
½ cent per £ (= ½ cent pr.)

Spot US dollars against sterling: $1.90 per £ ($1.9000)
3 months' forward: $1.90½ per £ ($1.9050)
i.e. dollars are at a discount of
½ cent per £ (= ½ cent dis.)

In other words, if forward dollars are more valued (i.e. at a premium), one gets fewer of them for a pound; if forward dollars are less valued (i.e. at a discount), one gets more of them for the pound.

In both cases the opposite would apply if seen from an American point of view: in the first example forward sterling would be at a discount of ½ cent (50 points) and in the second at a premium of ½ cent (50 points).

Cross rates

It is normal for customers to approach their bank's foreign exchange department to buy a foreign currency against their own or to sell a foreign currency against their own. There are, however, exceptions when for some reason one foreign currency is traded against another. Such deals are known as *cross deals* and the price that is quoted is known as a *cross rate*. Whereas there are many cross rates (Dutch guilders against Japanese yen, French francs against Spanish pesetas, etc.), the term 'the cross rate' has traditionally been reserved for the price of Canadian dollars in terms of US dollars.

It is worth bearing in mind that the cross rate depends on the viewpoint of the beholder; what might be a cross rate to an Italian, for example Swiss francs against Belgian francs, would not be a cross rate to either a Belgian or a Swiss.

Swaps

The word *swap* is well known and widely used, partly in connection with borrowing arrangements between central banks of different countries.

A swap is a pair of foreign exchange deals in the same two currencies but for different delivery dates and in opposite directions. Often both the deals constituting the pair are entered into by the same two partners, but this need not be so. The amounts involved will be identical for one of the currencies and similar for the other, the difference here being the result of the difference in exchange rates for different dates.

A swap for £100,000 against dollars, spot against forward, might consist of these two deals: on 1 February, A sells to B £100,000 for delivery on 3 February at $2.10 and buys from

B £100,000 for delivery on 3 May at $2.095. This is a swap. Both legs of it were done by A with the same partner, but in the second deal C could have taken the place of B and the pair of transactions would still have been a swap as far as A is concerned. The amount of dollars received by A on 3 February is $210,000 and the amount given by him on 3 May is only $209,500 because the dollar is at a premium (i.e. is more valuable) for forward delivery. In this example the amounts of one currency (sterling) are identical (£100,000), while the amounts of the other currency (dollars) are similar ($210,000 and $209,500).

Swaps take place between commercial customers and their bankers, or between banks, or between governments, when it is desired to move out of one currency into another for a limited period and without incurring the exchange risk of an open position in either of them. By doing the later deal at the same time as the earlier one, the exchange risk is avoided. This is useful when it is desired to alter the date of receipt or payment rather than cancel it altogether. The most obvious examples of this are those occurring when banks use swaps to match long and short positions which are identical in size but for different delivery dates, or when customers use swaps to move exchange contracts done some time ago on a forward basis from the original and provisional delivery date to the one actually required. The swaps arranged between central banks are, perhaps less obviously, a similar tool for changing the date rather than for altering the fact of payments due: they neither increase nor reduce the exchange risks involved in the country's balance-of-payments position, nor do they improve the reserves in real terms. They are, nevertheless, an attractive device for dealing short-term with an existing shortage of currency reserves.

A united market

The problem of language leads unfortunately and regrettably to misunderstandings. These do occur even though foreign exchange dealers take great trouble to avoid them by repeating what they believe they have done, in different words or in a different language, before the end of the telephone conversation. If in serious doubt, they confirm it on the telex before time has made a change in the rate probable.

Nevertheless, situations do occasionally arise in which two dealers sincerely and firmly believe different facts about the same conversation and contract. It has become quite common to tape-record telephonic deals, but if this has not been done or is not conclusive, it is usual and right to share equally the damage done to one or other of the parties and not to maintain an adamant belief in personal infallibility. The principle underlying this custom is that banks wish to continue to do foreign exchange business together and that this makes it necessary to respect the convictions, however mistaken, of one's partners.

The same desire for an agreeable business relationship in the longer run also explains why dealers will bargain hard and persistently but will never cheat their counterparts. Furthermore, they practise a measure of mutual help in professional difficulties which often astonishes outsiders: sometimes they do deals which do not suit them, merely to oblige a dealer in another country; at other times they will lean over backwards to assist a trainee dealer in another bank and to prevent his making a costly mistake.

These facts point to the solidarity of the foreign exchange community, to their spirit of eager yet friendly competition, and to their understandable enjoyment of an activity both exhausting and stimulating. The resulting loyalty to the profession and to its members is well summarized by the motto of the International Foreign Exchange Club: 'Once a dealer, always a dealer'.

3
SIX CHOICES

The businessman who has to divert some of his time to foreign exchange problems will sometimes need and seek information. Most often he will be confronted with actual choices and will be aware of the financial importance of deciding on the right course of action or inaction. Which dilemmas confront him will depend on whether he is concerned mainly with imports or with exports, with overseas investments, or with the purchase of raw materials or factory installations from abroad.

This chapter selects six of the most common of these choices or problems, not on the grounds that they are necessarily the most difficult or most interesting, but because they have the most relevance for the largest number of managing or financial directors in industrial and commercial firms.

Choice 1: Spot or forward?

Should those who have entered into a firm commercial commitment to buy from abroad and pay in foreign currency, or to sell abroad and receive foreign currency, cover the currency straight away on a forward basis or should they wait until the time of payment or receipt and then cover it on a spot basis?

Exchange control does in some countries restrict the businessman's choice. In others there is no such control at all or the exchange control regulations leave the choice to the individual or company: to cover forward or not to cover forward. It is therefore important to consider what factors should influence decisions in this matter.

Covering forward is a form of insurance. Those whose total reserves are low and for whom it is vital that the price of a particular installation or raw material or sale of goods shall not be affected adversely by a change in the exchange rate may see no alternative to covering forward. Costs and probabilities may both incline them to take the risk, but normal commercial prudence suggests that forward cover is necessary.

Many bankers expand this view to the admonition that all their customers should cover forward all commercial commitments. The arguments advanced in favour of this all-embracing rule are: (*a*) that the job of the customer is to think about his trade or production and not about foreign exchange; (*b*) that the banks provide a professional service which customers should use without involving themselves in difficult technical considerations. This view, while reasonable for the small business, is not tenable for the more sophisticated company with frequent and substantial involvement in international transactions. To such a company the argument is like not interviewing a prospective secretary because one's business is the manufacture of shoes and not the assessment of personnel.

If the decision – whether to cover forward or not – has to be taken, it would be helpful to have some general rules as a guide. Unfortunately, the needs of no two companies are identical, nor are the risks or the cost of cover the same in any 2 weeks of the year. It is, at best, possible to list some of the relevant questions to be asked and to suggest that they be answered and the decisions reviewed every few months, especially whenever a particularly big deal is contemplated or when an international development affecting currencies merits special attention.

1. Is it likely that the currency I have to buy will be upvalued or will float upwards before the time of payment (or that the currency I will have to sell will be devalued or will float downwards)?
2. Is my own currency likely to change its official parity or actual exchange rate against some, many or all foreign currencies or to float outside present limits?

Introduction to foreign exchange

3. Is the foreign currency or my own currency likely to be involved in any general realignment of rates during this period, such as occurs in the European Monetary System (EMS) from time to time?
4. How might the foreign currency or my own currency fare if there are further changes in the international monetary system, such as the introduction of new intervention points or the extension of floating rates or the re-fixing of now freely floating currencies?
5. What is the most that the changes feared (whether likely or unlikely to occur) will cost me: (*a*) as a percentage, (*b*) in actual cash.
6. What is the actual cost of forward cover (the difference between spot now and forward now): (*a*) as a percentage per annum and adjusted for the period I am concerned with, (*b*) in actual cash?[1]
7. What is (*a*) the likely and (*b*) the possible improvement or worsening in the spot rate between now and the end of the period?
8. Is the forward rate, as sometimes happens, actually more favourable than the spot rate, so that forward cover is desirable even though the risks (see questions 1 to 7) are deemed insufficient to justify insurance?

Nobody denies that it is difficult to answer these questions with any degree of accuracy. The costs of forward cover, and the losses consequent upon an exposed position, are such as to merit the most careful consideration in taking the appropriate decisions. These decisions do not always remain valid for long periods and therefore need frequent and careful review.

How to calculate the cost of forward cover

Spot sterling/dollar $2.0500
3 months' forward:
    seen from the UK: 1¾ – 1½ cents premium
    seen from the USA: 1¾ – 1½ cents discount

---

[1] If, for instance, 3 months' dollars cost an English importer 2.18 and spot dollars 2.1920, this amounts to a premium of about 2.20% per annum [(4×1.20)/2.18] or (adjusted for the period we are concerned with) ½% of the invoice amount. This is equivalent to 1.2 US cents per £, or about £5.450 on an invoice of $2,200,000.

Contracting to buy the dollars 3 months before payment therefore costs 1¾ cents more, i.e. $2.0325 are obtainable per pound (whereas the present rate for spot would yield $2.0500 and the actual rate for spot in 3 months' time is unknown). When the dollar is at a discount against sterling the reduced dollar receipt becomes an extra dollar receipt, but of course the real result of the decision – whether to cover forward or not – will still remain unknown until the 3 months have passed and the new spot rate is known.

The duty to cover forward
In an age of generally floating exchange rates and the resulting fluctuations in exchange rates, the profit on a commercial transaction which relies heavily on overseas raw materials or overseas sales can be wiped out or doubled. To ask the question 'Should we cover forward?' and to answer it correctly is therefore vital not only to the fate of a particular transaction but sometimes even to the very existence of a company. The banker therefore has both a right and a duty to advise his customer expertly and wisely in this matter. Companies should never take avoidable exchange risks.

The following principles should be applied to decisions in this area:

1. If you have already bought in one currency and have already sold in another currency, cover forward.
2. Deviate from 1 above if you see no danger ahead or only the likelihood of a change in your favour and if the amount is small in relation to your total trade. Deviate only if you are quite sure that your knowledge is sufficient and your advice good. Do this rarely and only in special circumstances.

   If, however, you have already bought in a currency and have yet to sell in another currency (or have already sold in one currency and have yet to buy in another currency), the decision whether you should obtain forward cover immediately or not is more difficult. If you regard an adverse change in the rate of exchange as likely, you will of course cover forward now. If on the other hand you expect no change, or even one which favours you, you may be justified in leaving the position open: if you cover at the wrong moment you enable a luckier competitor to ruin you. In this type of situation there is no moral merit in covering forward as against not covering forward: in either case you are taking an unavoidable risk which contains a large speculative element and is probably an inevitable part of your business.

Choice 2: Time options or swaps?

Those who cover their currency commitments by making purchases or sales of currency for forward delivery frequently have to face the fact that the exact date when the foreign currency will be needed (in the case of imports) or received (in the case of exports) is not known at the time when the commercial contract is signed and forward cover is arranged.

There exists a choice of methods to deal with this problem. The easiest way, although not usually the least costly, is to obtain from the bank a time option forward contract. This fixes the rate of exchange irrevocably but leaves the exact delivery date to be decided later by the customer. (As in all foreign exchange deals, the foreign currency and the domestic currency are paid on the same day, making a true exchange. The domestic currency is paid on the day when the foreign currency is really wanted, or received on the day on which the foreign currency becomes available.)

This is clearly advantageous, but not cheap. The customer has to pay the bank for the privilege of not fixing the delivery date when the foreign exchange deal is done; the cost of such an option contract is the premium or discount ruling at the time the contract is made for the most costly of the delivery dates within the customer's range.

For this reason the customer looks for an alternative way of covering forward, even though the exact date of delivery is unknown at the time the forward deal is done: this way is to cover forward for an arbitrarily selected but fixed date and later to adjust this by means of a swap. In most cases this proves cheaper than a time option contract.

The adjusting swap in fact consists of a pair of exchange deals between the customer and the banks and was described in some detail in Chapter 2. One half or 'leg' of the swap is for the delivery date of the original forward contract and is in the opposite direction. The other leg is for the desired new delivery date and is in the same direction as the original forward contract. Thus, the delivery date is moved from the presumptive to the actual date of payment or receipt.

The comparative advantages and disadvantages of time options on the one hand and of fixed contracts followed by swaps on the other are easily listed.

1. Time option contracts are costly, but they give complete protection against exchange risks. Fixed contracts followed by adjusting swaps give only partial protection, but tend to work out cheaper. Indeed, the only circumstances in which they present a risk are if the premium or discount changes adversely between the date of original contract and the date of adjustment. This occurs during periods of currency speculation or when interest rates in one of the two countries have changed considerably.
2. Both are fairly predictable in the short term. The cost of a swap for a short actual span of time rarely exceeds the cost of the time option for the longer presumed span of time. At the same time, however, a complete breakdown in the forward market could prevent the adjusting swap technique being used.

Those with a fair volume of business, adequate foreign exchange staff and the will to take small risks often show a preference for the fixed-date forward contract followed by an adjusting swap rather than for the generally dearer but safer time option contract.

Choice 3: Invoicing in one's own currency or in foreign currency?

In the foregoing paragraphs we were concerned with invoices (received or issued) in the currency of another country. Many firms buy and sell on the basis of contracts expressed in their own currency. This corresponds to old-established practice in many industries and saves both work and worry for one partner in such transactions: conversion into foreign currency is not his problem and exchange risks do not, on the face of it, concern him. Yet there are situations in which firms should consider currency invoicing as an alternative. Let us therefore examine the possible advantages of such a change.

Exports

The practice of issuing invoices in foreign currency for exports has received much publicity in recent years. Given certain conditions it can increase profitability by obtaining for the proceeds of goods a rate of exchange that is better than either the present spot rate or the likely future spot rate.

This is only true if (*a*) there is a reliable forward market for the currency in question; (*b*) the foreign currency is traded forward at a premium against the exporter's own currency; and (*c*) the exporter tends to receive payment a long time after the receipt of orders (which is when he is able to sell the proceeds forward). Clearly, a premium of 2% or 3% per annum makes currency invoicing coupled with forward sale of the proceeds more interesting than a premium of only ½% or 1% per annum. Equally, if a delay of 2 years between receipt of order and receipt of payment is expected, bigger savings may be shown through forward cover than would be the case over a period of only 3 or 6 months.

In any event, currency invoicing coupled with forward sale of the proceeds exposes the exporter to no greater exchange risk than invoicing in his own currency, provided of course that he is assured through sufficiently trained staff of prompt action in the forward market as soon as a commercial contract in foreign currency is entered into.

If however the buyer of the goods is alert to currency matters, he may prefer to be invoiced in the exporter's own currency so that he can buy it forward at a discount as soon as he has placed the order for the goods. The buyer would thus benefit from the differential between spot and forward, and prevent the seller from doing so.

Imports

It is even more interesting to analyse a transaction in the opposite direction, because one might at first sight assume that the importer who receives an invoice in his own currency has no worries and ought to be delighted about the simplicity of the paying procedure. There are, however, three situations which might cause him to regret that he has to pay in his own currency.

First, if the foreign currency which he considers a reasonable alternative to his own currency for a particular transaction happens to be at a substantial discount against his own currency, he can cheapen his imports by paying in that foreign currency and buying it forward. He does not usually add to his risks by doing so but there is likely to be a delay between his agreeing to be invoiced in a foreign currency and his actually receiving and accepting the quotation, a delay during which a change in forward rates could be damaging. It would therefore be wiser to ask for two quotations, one in his own currency and one in foreign currency and to calculate at the time of ordering which one would work out cheaper in real terms.

Second, if foreign suppliers are willing to invoice importers in the importer's own currency but insist on a guarantee against the effects of a devaluation of that currency, it is better to refuse to do so and to ask to be invoiced instead in a foreign currency which can be bought forward. An importer can, in the case of currency invoicing, insure against the risk of devaluation by covering forward; the consequences of the guarantee cannot always be avoided by a protecting deal in the forward market.

Third, many suppliers who are willing to invoice importers in the importer's currency remember previous devaluations and are fearful of the loss they would suffer if this calamity were to recur. They therefore add a percentage to the price per ton or per unit. Where this percentage is similar to the actual cost of forward cover at that moment there can be no great objection. It has been the experience of some large importers in such countries, however, that the percentage added has not been on that scale but in the region of five or ten times that (e.g. 5% per annum instead of ½% per annum). Such terms have been proposed on the grounds that they might well represent the cost of forward cover by the time the supplier realized that a renewed crisis was imminent. In such cases it is clearly better for the importer to accept invoices in a foreign currency for which there is an adequate forward market and to buy such forward cover if he sees fit. If he is situated near one of the world's larger foreign exchange markets, he should be able to judge the risks much better and buy cover in most instances far more cheaply than some of his suppliers.

Hard currencies

When one's own currency is traded forward at a premium it is the importer, not the exporter, who can enhance his profits by offering to pay in the supplier's currency; if that currency is traded forward at a discount (as, for instance, sterling generally used to be against the US dollar or the German mark), he can buy it forward as soon as he has ordered the goods and can thus get it more cheaply.

A hypothetical transaction looks as follows, assuming payment by a German importer for British goods due 1 year after ordering the goods.

Sterling price	= £1,000 per ton
Discount for 1 year sterling (about 4% p.a.)	= 17 Pfennig per £
Spot £/DM rate	= DM4.20 per £
Forward £/DM rate	= DM4.03 per £
Spot price per ton	= DM4,200
Forward price per ton	= DM4,030
Saving on 1,000 tons if the spot rate does not drop	= DM170,000
Saving on 1,000 tons if the spot rate drops to DM4.10 per £	= DM70,000
Loss on 1,000 tons if the spot rate drops to DM4.00 per £	= DM30,000

The decision whether to cover forward or not will of course depend only in part on the estimated likelihood of the spot sterling rate moving during the year. The importer will be aware that contracting to pay in foreign currency and covering the currency commitment forward is safe (as safe as contracting to pay in his own currency) and may be profitable, whereas contracting to pay in foreign currency and not covering the currency commitment forward involves an exchange risk.

Choice 4: Do banks advise or merely serve?

There is a considerable divergence of opinion among bankers and their customers as to the precise role of the foreign exchange departments of the banks. Their main function is undeniably to serve their customers by buying and selling foreign exchange whenever required, at reasonable rates and in a way which minimizes the risks, troubles and delays which might befall those whose business involves foreign exchange. This service is of a high degree of excellence and can be obtained from a very large number of banks. Volume of turnover, geographical specialization and the excellence of individual foreign exchange dealers may, at times, give certain houses a marginal advantage over others, but all banks will act quickly and obtain similar rates because the foreign exchange market is organized to make this possible. Information about the borrowing and lending of foreign currencies, exchange control regulations in various countries, payment methods, existing rates, the availability of forward cover and any other factual aspects of foreign exchange will all be readily available. Permission will be obtained where necessary, payments reliably and speedily made. Service is the aim and this aim is achieved.

Some banks also offer advice on whether forward cover should be taken or not, or on whether transactions should be speeded up or delayed because of probable changes in the rate of exchange of the currencies chosen for purchases or sales. Other banks try to avoid doing so, explaining that their duty is to do what their customers ask them to do efficiently, speedily and cheaply and not to tell the customers what to ask them to do. This unwillingness to include real advice in the service offered is justified by arguments which are varied and generally valid. The banks are rightly afraid of being misrepresented or misinterpreted. They regard it as a presumption to appear definite in matters which are merely opinions and in areas which are exceedingly difficult to assess. They believe that businessmen must take their own decisions and that they cannot delegate this obligation.

All this is true. The difficulty seems to arise from a misunderstanding of the concept of advice. No sensible person would expect bankers to tell customers what to do or customers blindly to obey such orders. Rather, customers should seek the opinions of the foreign exchange experts in the bank, which ought surely to be, if not wiser, at least much deeper than those which most customers can hope to form during a daily routine which is much more remote from the professional currency world. The professionals ought to be able and willing to offer such opinions to customers readily, clearly and fairly. This service should be an essential part of the work of a good foreign exchange department. It is obvious that the customer, having heard what one or several professionals have to say, will make up his own mind and will buy or not buy, or sell or not sell (of course within the actual regulations and market possibilities). The bank advises; the customer decides; the bank then acts on his behalf.

Choice 5: Loyalty or selection?

Those having to buy or sell foreign exchange, especially for forward delivery, sometimes wonder whether they should obtain and accept quotations from only one bank and hope that they are being looked after as loyal customers of long standing, or whether they should 'shop around', asking several banks for quotations each time and accepting the best, possibly after prolonged and vigorous argument with several of them.

The advantage of 'shopping around' is that it keeps customer and banker in a healthily competitive frame of mind. In extreme cases it discloses grossly exaggerated dealing margins habitually claimed by a very small minority of banks. In most cases it unearths only slight variations, particularly where quotations for spot delivery are concerned.

When rates fluctuate violently, which often happens where there is a system of floating exchange rates, comparisons are meaningful only if they are simultaneous: even a 1-minute difference between the times of two enquiries may invalidate this exercise.

A further snag about 'shopping around' is that it costs money. A firm in the north of England wishing to buy $42,000 spot and telephoning to three London banks will thereby involve itself in at least six telephone calls (three to ask for a quote, three more to accept or reject it), each of several minutes' duration. One may reasonably hope to get an improvement of two points in the rate, say from 2.1020 to 2.1022, which would save less than £2.[2] Even this hope may not always be fulfilled. When it is, it hardly pays the telephone charges, still less the salary of the senior executive who handled the matter. Few firms, in their commendable eagerness to get the best possible rates, seem to calculate this.

It is also the experience of those who 'shop around' that, after a while, none of the dealers approached give quite the same detailed attention to them as they do to those who accept less critically and rely more obviously upon the services of their own bank.

That the blandishments – in the form of superlatively attractive exchange rates – which are sometimes used to lure foreign exchange customers from their present bank, cannot and are not kept up once the customer has been won over is the sad experience of many an over-eager executive. He may well appreciate also, when it is too late, the apparent effortlessness with which his regular bankers carried out complicated payment instructions.

We must conclude that it is right and expedient to 'shop around' at times, both to confirm that one is adequately looked after by one's own bank and to assure oneself of the best rate in a particular case. However, this is worth doing

[2] $42,000 = £20,000. The difference between 2.1020 and 2.1022 (2 points) amounts to 40,000 points or 400 US cents or US$4 on this amount.

only for items of an exceptional nature or size, although what may seem large for many firms is, as the above example shows, not big enough in foreign exchange terms to merit expensive checking on every occasion.

A final word of warning is perhaps not out of place before leaving this topic. When customers ask banks to hold a spot exchange rate firm for even 5 minutes, they are forcing a dealer who knows his job to take an additional margin of several points to provide himself with a cushion against violent short-term movements in the rate. The result for the customer tends to be that the best of three rates obtained on a 'good for 5 minutes' basis (enabling him to shop around at leisure) is worse for him than the worst of three rates obtained on a 'for immediate reply' basis.

Choice 6: Financial futures: hedging or gambling?

Futures markets in commodities such as wheat or cocoa have a long history on both sides of the Atlantic. Their main purpose is and should be to protect traders and manufacturers against adverse movements in price due to crop failures, political upheavals or economic crises.

By selling or buying on a futures market long before they are ready to sell or buy physical goods they can, in effect, insure themselves against future price changes. When they are ready to sell or buy the physical goods they reverse the original futures deal: the profit or loss on that will be similar and opposite to the amount by which the price for physical goods (or spot delivery) falls short of or exceeds the expected price. Done expertly and within proper limits it works like any insurance and is not dissimilar to forward deals in the foreign exchange market: it acts as a hedge.

In recent years the same facilities have been rapidly extended into the financial field. These financial futures have both gained considerable publicity and been traded in ever-growing amounts. Futures trading in currencies provides an alternative to forward dealing and thus improves the market available to importers and exporters.

Futures trading in Treasury Bills and other paper offers a

unique opportunity of hedging (insuring) against adverse changes in the rate of interest. In periods of violently and unpredictably fluctuating interest rates this can be of considerable help to borrowers and lenders alike.

Many futures markets are organized in such a way as to guarantee effectively the standing of the participants through a system of margins. In this way they provide a far-reaching though not absolute assurance of delivery which is of course lacking in the traditional foreign exchange market. The time may come when the magnitude of exchange rate fluctuations and the consequent danger of default through exchange losses will force the foreign exchange market to adopt a similar system of cash margins for forward deals. Between banks and customers this was widely done in the thirties. Between banks and banks it would constitute a revolutionary but wholesome innovation.

How far financial futures should be traded by financial institutions, commercial firms and even individuals raises profound questions of business morality. The decision must be left to financial management in the changing light of actual circumstances, but the following answer can surely be accepted as a general rule which should not be abandoned or ignored without very good reasons.

Futures markets furnish us with an excellent way of reducing the intrinsic and inevitable risks to which the price mechanism in a free economy exposes our chosen field of manufacture or trade. This is called hedging. If, however, they are used in the expectation of finding a source of independent profit, participation is much more speculative and can be described as gambling.

Choice 7: Currency options: an essential tool in certain situations

A number of futures exchanges on both sides of the Atlantic now offer currency options. Helped by their quotations, banks are able to write currency option contracts for their customers in most major currencies, for any specific amounts and any chosen date.

A currency option contract gives the holder the right to

receive and pay for a currency at a fixed forward date (a call option) or to deliver and be paid for a currency at a fixed forward date (a put option).

Whereas normal foreign exchange contracts (whether for spot or for forward delivery) are binding on both parties, and therefore give the customer both the right and the duty to deliver, this is not true with currency option contracts: the party which has 'written the option' has the duty but not the right to deliver; the other party (the customer) has the right but not the duty to deliver. For this right the customer pays a fee (called 'option premium'), which is non-returnable and which depends on both the length of time for which he has the right to deliver or receive currency, and how remote the price is from present market prices at which he has that right.

Currency options are useful to firms which have to tender for projects in a foreign currency or to those who may be committing themselves under some other heading to transactions in a foreign currency. Costing calculations are impossible until it is established in which currency the contract will materialize, but such calculations must be completed before negotiations begin. A currency option makes this possible.

A normal forward contract when tendering is as risky as tendering and not covering forward: if the tender is accepted and no forward contract has been arranged, a period of uncovered exchange rate exposure has to be endured; if the tender is unsuccessful, the forward currency contract has to be reversed at market rates, which can result in an exchange loss or profit of unpredictable magnitude. On the other hand, the currency option contract limits the possible loss to the size of the option premium already paid. It is the appropriate tool to use.

For most companies, however, currency option contracts are inappropriate where a firm commercial contract already exists. Some professionals with suitable skills and experience use them as an alternative to ordinary forward exchange or financial futures contracts in specific situations.

4
MONEY ACROSS FRONTIERS

The theory of interest arbitrage

This chapter deals with the interrelationship between the foreign exchange market and the money market and between foreign exchange rates and interest rates. It revolves around the *theory of interest arbitrage*.

The theory of interest arbitrage states that interest rates for comparable short-term investments in different countries and currencies must differ by the same amount as the spot exchange rate differs from the forward exchange rate. It does not say that the exchange rate difference follows the interest rate difference, nor that the interest rate difference follows the exchange rate difference; all it says is that a change in either of them will be reflected by a corresponding change in the other. This is a startling statement with important practical consequences. It is true and therefore worthy of closer examination.

When an investor or saver, company treasurer or bank cashier, or any other holder of liquid funds, considers how best to employ them, his foremost consideration will be the safety of his money. He needs to be certain that the standing of the borrower is such as to remove any reasonable fear of default. In certain parts of the world he will also have to take into account the possibility of political changes restricting the potential borrower's freedom to repay. Only when these factors have been examined and judged can the lender legitimately interest himself in the comparative return on his money offered to him by different types of borrowers, or indeed by different borrowers of similar type.

Within a single country this is the way short-term money is placed. However, when borrower and lender are situated in different countries, or more precisely in different currency areas, an added complication arises: one of the two has to operate in a foreign currency and must therefore bear, throughout the period of the loan, the risks of an adverse change in the exchange rate. If the lender insists on lending his own currency, then the borrower will worry lest the currency borrowed appreciates before he repays, thus making the borrowing more expensive than the rate of interest taken by itself. If the borrower is able to insist on borrowing and owing the money in terms of his own currency and this currency loses in comparative value before he repays, then the lender will receive back less of his own currency than he lent; the total return on his money would in this case be less than the agreed rate of interest.

In the face of these facts it is surprising how many people still believe that vast short-term funds move to another currency area in response to a marginally higher rate of interest. Changes in domestic rates certainly have some influence in attracting or not attracting foreign money, or in allowing domestic funds to be tempted or not tempted to go abroad. The extent to which this happens is, however, much less than is often implied by statements made at times of currency crisis or when interest rates change. Most managers of short-term funds would not feel justified in exposing themselves to the risk of a change in exchange rates. The unexpected occurrence, or at least unpredictable timing, of recent changes in exchange rates has caused losses to those whose funds crossed currency frontiers without precautions, losses which have been substantial enough to make this practice less and less common. 'Hot money' of this kind is not the regular feature of money markets which it once was, and commentators should recognize this. Nowadays big movements of money across frontiers are more often motivated by expectations of a favourable change in the rate of exchange than by the additional earning prospect of a higher rate of interest.

Covered arbitrage

What then happens normally? Lenders who wish to place

funds in another country, and therefore in another currency, can insure themselves against the attendant exchange risks not only by buying the relevant foreign currency for immediate delivery, but also by selling at the same time that foreign currency on the forward market. Provided the cost of this insurance (namely, the difference between the spot and the forward rate) does not exceed the extra interest they can earn by the transfer, the lender would proceed with the investment 'on a covered basis'; that is to say, he would buy spot and sell forward the foreign currency at the same time as fixing the lending in foreign currency.

The theory of interest arbitrage states that this cannot happen. Practice shows that it does. This apparent contradiction may best be explained by a comparison with the world of physics.

If two tanks containing water are connected by a pipe at their lowest point and if this pipe is of sufficient diameter and kept clear, its presence will make possible the flow of water from one tank to the other and will ensure that the water in both tanks is always at the same level, although this level will vary every time water is taken from or added to the system. It does not matter in which section of the system alterations are made; whichever tank is affected, a balancing effect will be transferred to the other. It is thus true to say that equilibrium is ensured, making the two water levels identical, and that this must always be so. It is also true, however, that water will move in one or the other direction through the pipe whenever an addition or removal of water from one tank has temporarily made the water levels disparate; the movement of water through the pipe is a precondition of the normal equilibrium of water levels (when there is not movement through the pipe) and not, in fact, a contradiction of it.

In the case of money, the following comments similarly apply.

1. The theory of interest arbitrage confirms that forward cover can make overseas short-term investment immune from exchange risks.

2. Forward deals will be done in simple response to interest rate impulses whenever the interest rate gain is more than the cost of forward cover.
3. Money will move immediately and in large amounts whenever this is true.
4. The existence of this possibility of moving short-term funds from one centre to another guarantees that rate advantages will be fully utilized at once and will stop being used only when the movement has affected demand and supply for the money, or for the foreign currency involved, to such an extent that the rate ceases to be attractive.
5. There is here a mechanism for establishing and maintaining equilibrium, akin to the physical mechanism of the connected water tanks.
6. Only minor advantages can exist, and very minor gains be expected, from moving funds on a covered basis.
7. The return on lending funds to borrowers of similar standing in any major currency must, after taking into account the cost or benefit of forward cover, be identical.

Practice versus theory

All this is true, and yet funds move. There are two groups of causes for this.

1. The 'water pipe', so to speak, may be too small to take the traffic, and adjustment may be delayed; quite often a change in rates is so sudden and so large that the new equilibrium can be reached only after a considerable movement of funds. Such re-deployment of money tends to cause liquidity problems and meets with resistance from the institutions involved, so that a delay occurs.
2. It is also possible for the 'water pipe' to be clogged up with 'dirt' to inhibit the free flow of water; many countries limit the allowed movement of short-term funds out of their own money market into foreign

money markets or vice versa. This too will delay the otherwise automatic process of re-establishing equilibrium.

Even if neither of these delaying factors operated there would still be money moving in large amounts across frontiers. The reason for this is that professional managers of money must seek optimum returns for their cash and will therefore regard even an extra $\frac{1}{32}$% per annum for a few weeks on a large amount of money as worth having. Such slight differences may arise because a special demand for money in a particular currency, or for a forward deal with a specific commercial background, puts a slight temporary pressure on one currency. Often these circumstances are known to only one bank and it will therefore enable that bank to improve the return on its or its customer's money on that particular day.

It is thus true that, as with the water tanks, two apparently contradictory statements are both valid. Interest arbitrage assures us of a situation of equilibrium and removes at normal times the chance of profit from moving money abroad without incurring an exchange risk. On the other hand, some such movement, obviously in response to the profit motive does take place and it is this which makes the achievement and maintenance of equilibrium possible. In the case of the water tanks the water levels are always equal, but only because water keeps flowing through the pipe whenever levels become unequal. In the case of money, the theory of interest arbitrage ensures a static location of funds which are to be invested without exchange risk, but only because funds do move as soon as this static situation no longer exists.

Hot money

Once the theory of interest arbitrage is accepted as true and seen to be confirmed by the actual relationship of interest rates and forward exchange rates from day to day, its various and far-reaching consequences become apparent. Two of these need to be mentioned.

Changes in discount rate or in other government-controlled

interest rates, decided upon not for reasons to do with domestic credit but because it is desired to alter the currency reserves by a change in the flow of inward or outward short-term investments, are effective only in so far as those who control funds are undisturbed by exchange risks and do not cover forward. For all others, the interest arbitrage calculation is relevant and the actual level of interest rates (taken by itself) is not.

It has already been suggested that fewer and fewer professional managers of money when placing funds look only to interest rates and completely ignore the risks inherent in an open position in foreign currency. That some still take this kind of risk is evident from responses to recent changes in interest rates, but it is not possible to assert simply that funds come in when rates are raised and go out again when they are lowered. Sometimes even the reverse happens.

We must therefore accept that the use of the interest arbitrage mechanism by so many professional managers of money makes it imperative for governments to find some way, other than merely the increasing of domestic interest rates, to attract foreign funds if they wish to bolster reserves temporarily. Governments often wish to do this, although they are inclined to scoff at the result of their deeds by calling money thus attracted 'hot money', the adjective having become pejorative in this connection. No doubt it is the fickleness of such funds rather than their existence which is deplored.

There are three main ways of attracting and keeping short-term funds, apart from the old-fashioned and often ineffective way of paying 'over the odds' for them. The most obvious and best way, but also the hardest, is to organize the domestic economy in such a manner that funds are brought in on a sustained wave of confidence. The growth of such an economy ensures good dividends, and the resulting stability of the currency, although probably resulting in low returns on fixed interest deposits, still attracts these because of the absence of devaluation fears and of the presence of revaluation hopes. This state of affairs is within the reach of any industrialized country, the citizens of which have normal good sense and a healthy political and social attitude.

The second way to attract funds or prevent their departure is by exchange control. This is, at worst, a locking of doors where the wish to cross thresholds ought not to exist. At best, it is an adequate way of coping with a nation's persistent failure to provide the social climate and economic growth which ought to be achieved to make such restrictive measures unnecessary. Some countries prevent the departure of foreign-owned funds by restricting the homeward remittance of dividends or the borrowing of local currency by foreign-owned subsidiaries. Others merely restrict the outward movement of resident-controlled monies. Any of these steps ease the task of keeping the reserves intact.

The third way is subtler, less permanent and less damaging to long-term industrial planning than exchange control. It involves intervention by the central bank in forward exchange rates. By this step the difference between spot and forward rates, and therefore the cost of forward cover, can be amended and the interest arbitrage calculation kept artificially out of equilibrium. It is like an official continuously pouring water into one of our two water tanks because it has been decided to power a government mill with the resultant flow of water. It can be done and it has been done. The only snag is that no central bank can go on giving or taking foreign currency in large amounts for ever; eventually the day of reckoning will come and the need to reverse the deals will aggravate the situation unless underlying conditions, such as the trade balance or confidence in the currency, have changed meanwhile.

The meaning and significance of forward rates

The other important consequence of the interest arbitrage doctrine is that, because it teaches us that forward rates affect interest rates and interest rates affect forward rates, we can no longer allege that the forward premium or discount of a currency reflects accurately the faith or lack of faith which people have in that currency. Such faith may, of course, find expression in the forward rate and there are many examples to confirm this. It is, however, a far less reliable indicator of the extent of such feeling among operators (including commercial customers as well as bankers and speculators) than is often supposed. Only if interest rates for at least one of the two currencies are completely flexible and uncontrolled by the authorities or by liquidity considerations can sentiment affecting the currency relationship be fully and accurately reflected via interest rates in the forward premium or discount. As soon as interest rates are affected by other influences it must follow that the forward premium or discount cannot fully express sentiment about future currency values. There are many illustrations to substantiate this point, the best-known of which is perhaps the growth of the discount for the pound sterling immediately after devaluation in 1967. At that time the risk of a further devaluation was minimal so soon after the first, yet the insurance against this eventuality had doubled in cost. The reason was a 2% increase in bank rate. Only the doctrine of interest arbitrage can explain this effect.

Interest arbitrage and business transactions

This then is the meaning of interest arbitrage for the importer or exporter: that forward rates do not necessarily, and rarely accurately, reflect the risks involved. Because the forward cover, unlike any other insurance cost, has no actuarial relationship to the risks, the businessman must ask himself two separate sets of questions when deciding whether to insure himself against the exchange risks of any particular international deal.

1. He has first to consider whether to cover the currency forward immediately after signing the commercial contract or whether to cover the currency spot when the time of payment comes, or whether to stay uncovered temporarily and review the situation once a week or once a month. He must thus ask himself whether he wishes to carry the exchange risks un-

insured, which will depend upon his estimate of the currency situation and also on the financial importance to his business of any loss that might occur.
2. If he estimates the risks to be great and the possible losses to be crippling for his business, he will have to proceed to the second set of questions which concerns the cost of cover. This cost, as we have seen, may be greater or less than the insurance premium he would deem appropriate. A 50:50 chance of a 10% change in the rate might justify an insurance cost of up to 5%, but in foreign exchange it could work out at 2% or 12%. In the latter case the businessman must accept the inevitable, remain uninsured, regret his earlier commercial contract and rely on prayer and hope. In the former he will insure by covering forward, grateful that money market forces (whether natural or government-induced) have caused an interest arbitrage situation which keeps the forward rates below the level which they might otherwise have reached.

The doctrine of interest arbitrage therefore adds a burden of thought and decision to the life of the sophisticated businessman engaged in international trade of any kind. Not only must he decide, and decide for himself, in the particular situation of the moment whether cover is necessary and whether the cost of cover is appropriate. He must further accept that sometimes forward cover is cheaper than the likely cost of covering spot at a later time, so that he will enter the forward market not only to reduce risks but also to increase profits. His earlier decision whether to invoice or to be invoiced in his own currency or in a foreign currency will likewise depend on what he is likely to do about forward cover if he has chosen foreign currency invoicing.

Summary
The interrelationship of the money market and the foreign exchange market, too often ignored and too little understood, and contained in the doctrine of interest arbitrage, creates problems and poses difficult questions for the business executive. At the same time it opens to him a field of

opportunity and profitability which to ignore is like manufacturing without accountancy or selling without public relations: forward cover has its problems, but it can be a source of real opportunity.

An actual example
1. The pound spot and forward.
    US close spot 2.2650–2.2660.★   3 months 0.90–1.00 dis.★
2. Eurocurrency interest rates.
    3 months sterling 12½–12⅝ p.a.★
    3 months US dollar 14–14¼ p.a.★
    (★See the foreign exchange report in one of the daily papers.)

Therefore:

3. Does it pay to turn sterling into dollars and deposit as dollars?

    Cost (loss of earnings in sterling) 12½% p.a. ⎫ 14¼% p.a.
    Cost of swap   1¾% p.a. ⎬
    Interest offered for US dollars   14% p.a. ⎭

    The US dollar deposit is ¼% p.a. less attractive than the sterling deposit.

4. Does it pay to turn dollars into sterling and deposit as sterling?

    Cost (loss of earnings in dollars)   14%
    Profit on swap   1.58% ⎫ approx.
    Interest offered for sterling   12½%   ⎬ 14¹⁄₁₆%

    It is just worth while turning dollars into sterling but the extra (¹⁄₁₆% or just over) might be eroded by expenses (telephone in making the arrangements, brokerage, cost of confirming and of payment orders, own time).

5. Method of calculation:
    (a) For 3: 1.00 cent (discount asked for 3 months) multiplied by 4 (to turn 3 months into 12 months) and then divided by number of dollars obtainable per pound for spot date viz. 2.2650.
    (b) For 4: 0.90 cent (discount offered for 3 months) multiplied by 4 (to turn 3 months into 12 months) and then divided by number of dollars needed (2.2660) to buy one pound for spot date.

Money across frontiers 47

.6. How to check (5):
   (a) *1% p.a.* of $2.26 is 2.26 cent or *226 points*.
   (b) 90 or 100 points (0.90 cent or 1.00 cent) multiplied by 4 is *360 points* or *400 points*. This is therefore approx. 1⅝% and 1¾% respectively (i.e. 226 = 1%, 360 = approx. 1.6%, 400 = approx. 1.8%).

5
BRETTON WOODS AND AFTER

The Bretton Woods Conference in July 1944 revised the international monetary system. Close international collaboration was to ensure stable exchange rates while allowing a measure of flexibility and adequate scope for the operation of free foreign exchange markets.

The International Monetary Fund was to have both more authority and more money than the Bank for International Settlements, which had been the first truly international monetary institution and which had operated with a considerable measure of success during the inter-war period.

The International Monetary Fund was set up to give aid to countries which, because of long-term changes or because of some temporary difficulty in the domestic economic scene, were short of foreign currency reserves. An elaborate system of rights and duties was designed. Funds were made available from the member countries sufficient to deal with most foreseeable situations of this kind. As the years passed, these funds have been increased substantially and indeed have proved to be generally sufficient as various international currency crises developed.

The problem of endowing the central organization with a necessary measure of authority was a more difficult one to solve, and undoubtedly has been only partially resolved. Certain undertakings have to be given by countries when borrowing from the International Monetary Fund, but it is arguable that these undertakings are not of a very definite kind, and that very little can be done by the International Monetary Fund if they are not honoured. The Letters of Intent which have so often been discussed in the past are part of this machinery of compulsion. They are formal undertakings by sovereign states to take definite measures to correct adverse trends in the domestic economy when borrowings from the International Monetary Fund exceed certain limits in size or duration.

Intervention points

The key to the system devised at Bretton Woods was that exchange rates should be allowed to fluctuate only within narrow limits set by so-called 'intervention points'. Each country, having fixed a parity against the United States dollar and also defined it in terms of gold, was committed to allowing fluctuations only within a margin not exceeding 1% either side of that parity, and then to intervene whenever pressures in the market looked like pushing the exchange rate outside that bracket. In December 1971 this margin was increased to 2¼%.

For most countries, the 1% margin had been sufficiently wide to allow for the normal fluctuations due to seasonal conditions and to temporary changes in the domestic economic situation. For a few, such as Canada, it tended to be too small to take account of the pressures on the demand and supply of foreign currency which occur from either commercial or investment causes. There was therefore considerable discussion for some years as to the desirability of widening the allowable margin for some countries or for all.

In the system of so-called *fixed exchange rates* it is clearly desirable to allow margins which will make pressure on the currency at either the top or the bottom intervention point fairly rare. It is arguable that the fluctuations which do normally occur in the foreign exchange market will tend to be greater if the allowed fluctuation is greater. It is possible that, in the absence of regular intervention at intermediate levels by the central bank, a larger allowed margin of fluctuation results merely in larger actual fluctuations, causing greater uncertainty to traders and investors and not in fact avoiding unpleasant weeks of real pressure at the intervention point which cause so much distress to those in charge of the national currency.

A practice developed during the years following the establishment of the International Monetary Fund and of the free foreign exchange markets (which had been closed for so long before, during and after the years of war). Central banks intervened not only at the intervention points, when the law required them to do so, but also at interim levels, in the interests of monetary management and the stability of the national currency. Considerable collaboration has developed in recent years between central banks in this practice, which was described in Chapter 1.

Intervention in the forward market

Certain central banks have at times also intervened in the forward exchange markets. Intervention in the forward exchange markets has always been a topic for considerable dispute. Some would maintain that this is an essential mechanism both for steadying the foreign exchange markets and, because of the importance of the theory of interest arbitrage, for managing domestic interest rates and the flow, inwards and outwards, of money. While there is much to be said in favour of occasional intervention in the forward exchange market with the aim of controlling the inward or outward flow of funds and the availability of credit inside the country, the intervention sometimes practised on a substantial scale at times of currency crises, with the aim of reducing the pressure of speculation, is open to more doubt.

Its main disadvantages are the following: first, it tends to make the task of the speculator easier by cheapening the cost if he is mistaken, without seriously reducing the profit if he is right; and second, it tends to put a considerable burden on the intervening central bank in terms of cost. Admittedly, if the speculation is unjustified, there is profit for the central bank in this operation, but if the speculation turns out to be justified and the calamity which people expect actually occurs, then it is at the expense of the central bank that the speculators reap their profits. The view is often taken by central banks therefore (with a degree of modesty which may be only partially based on fact) that they ought not to act as if they are sure of the stability of their own currency when the whole world seems to be of a different opinion. Certainly, the substantial intervention by the British authorities before the devaluation in 1967 in the forward exchange market added greatly to the loss which the Bank of England incurred as a result of that devaluation.

Intervention in the spot market

Intervention by central banks for spot delivery at times of fluctuations and of general commercial pressures has become an established practice. This clearly serves a useful purpose, although many dealers in the foreign exchange market are disturbed at the unexpected timing of such intervention and the difficulty which it tends to create in forecasting developments in exchange rates.

If the role of foreign exchange dealers in making and keeping a healthy market for the benefit of the commercial and investing community is a real one, then anything which makes their task more difficult or more risky has to be considered with extreme caution. Apart from this, the intervention by the central banks in the market for immediate or spot delivery is useful and has become part of the monetary system.

The basis for such intervention lies in a simple fact. When a change in the relationship of demand and supply for any foreign currency puts pressure on the exchange rate, this rate will change, unless some central authority removes the surplus supply or satisfies the excess demand by intervening and putting into the market some of the foreign currency in its own stock (currency reserves) or by taking the excess supply of such currency into its stock. At the intervention points, in a fixed-rate system, the central bank has no choice but to take currency into its stock or give currency from its stock. At all interim levels, however, and when floating rates are in operation, it has a choice either to do this or to let the change in the demand–supply relationship cause a movement in the exchange rate.

A government and its central bank must consider whether a growth in the reserves is more important than a splendid rate of exchange, or vice versa, and whether at times of pressure it is better to let the reserves drop or to let the exchange rate drift downwards. It is that decision which determines whether the central bank intervenes in the market.

There are of course moments when central banks intervene in the foreign exchange market for much less official reasons: either to carry through an operation on behalf of a government department, or simply to test the market (see Chapter 1).

The function performed by the exchange dealers of central banks in understanding and guiding the foreign exchange markets is one which must not be underestimated. It is a field in which the central banks have had a most beneficial effect on the re-establishment and organization of the post-war exchange markets, and one which dealers have reason to know and value.

The philosophy and its effects

The system of Bretton Woods proved beneficial to the growth of economic prosperity in the Western world. It was based on fixed parities and relatively narrow dealing margins, guarded on either side by an intervention point, with substantial aid available to member countries from central funds against relatively limited undertakings to put matters right as soon as possible.

This was coupled with the general philosophy that changes in parity should not be delayed if they were justified, but should not be made every time the economic situation at home required adjustment or further control. It also made possible substantial aid to less developed countries from richer and more successful nations.

Nevertheless, both the plight still continuing in the Third World and the outbreak of sometimes severe and almost crippling international currency crises in the Western world have from time to time inflamed discussion as to the merits and defects of the Bretton Woods system, as embodied in the International Monetary Fund and its sister organizations. Most of the criticisms of the Bretton Woods system ought, in truth, to have been addressed to the member countries rather than to the Fund itself.

The main criticism has centred on the relative rigidity of the Bretton Woods system, because whenever a crisis broke out the focal point of the struggle for maintaining the parity was the intervention point. It was only natural to question the very existence of such intervention points and to advocate a system either devoid of intervention points or with a greater possibility of moving them when pressure builds up.

The change to floating

If there are no parities fixed between the currencies of the world, then rates can float freely; at no particular point is the central bank obliged to interfere. Few people seriously advocate that central banks should not be allowed to intervene in the foreign exchange markets: the social consequences of a decline or improvement in the exchange rate, together with its effect on the prices of imports and exports, are matters of governmental concern in a modern community. There are, however, many who prefer the choice of those points to be left to the government of the country and not fixed for years ahead. With such an arrangement the rate is allowed to move or not as the government sees fit. While this is an attractive idea in principle, the problems attendant upon it are such that the International Monetary Fund and its main members resolutely declined to contemplate it until the 1970s.

In 1971 most major countries resorted temporarily to floating exchange rates. The Smithsonian Settlement in December of that year brought the world back to the system of fixed parities, albeit in a slightly amended form. After the second devaluation of the US dollar in 1973, floating rates were again adopted by many countries. The 1978 amendments to the Statutes of the International Monetary Fund accepted and permitted this practice which many countries continue to use. Some of them now regard it as good in itself. Many more accept it as a second best made unavoidable because domestic economic upheavals and violent changes in world commodity prices (oil above all) make the system of more permanently fixed parities impossible to operate.

Crawling pegs

Before *managed floating* became common in the seventies, academics sought a system which would give a measure of certainty to those who needed fixed rates to enable them to plan their future activities and yet provide that system with a mechanism for change to add some flexibility to it.

Most members of the International Monetary Fund had for years taken the view that the system of fixed parities and intervention points made a major contribution to the peaceful development of international trade, but that greater flexibility ought to be achieved. One suggestion was that when a currency is under pressure (in either direction) the intervention points could be moved a small way in the appropriate direction at the end of an accounting period of 3 or 6 months. This concept of slow devaluation became known as the *crawling peg* system.

Some people are in favour of automatic adjustment at the end of the accounting period – the so-called mandatory crawling peg. Others would rather leave it up to the government whether or not to make use of this facility – the system known as the voluntary crawling peg. Of both these systems one can say that they cause considerable confusion and a great deal of work without solving any real problems. If the pressure on a currency is really great enough to cause concern, then a ½% or 1% adjustment of its exchange rate does not serve any useful purpose. If there are rumours circulating that a devaluation or revaluation in the order of 5%, 10% or 15% is needed and if such a correction is in fact being considered seriously, then the rate adjustments permitted by the crawling peg system do little to restore confidence.

Nevertheless, many variants of the crawling peg idea have been tried and in some cases have functioned satisfactorily. New Zealand operates a type of crawling peg. The periodic adjustments in the European Monetary System follow a similar pattern, although less formally.

Monetary reform

The Bretton Woods system, created in 1944, was developed with considerable skill and expertise by the leading financial experts of the world. It lived up to the demands of a quarter of a century and has been an effective weapon in the struggle for prosperity. In the last decade changes were forced upon the system by the world economic crisis, energy supply problems and the new status of the dollar.

If not everything hoped for had actually been achieved, this was not the system's fault. The achievement of international monetary stability and economic growth called for further developments, new institutions and an open mind on the part of the member countries.

After some years of disruptive foreign exchange crises and discussions at top international level (such as the Morse Committee of the Group of Twenty or the monthly meetings of governors of central banks at Basle), the Statutes of the International Monetary Fund were altered on 1 April 1978. The most important change made in 1978 permitted floating of currencies. It is now up to individual member countries whether to equip their currencies with fixed or floating parities and how to define the relationship of their currencies to those of other countries.

It is still the fundamental principle of foreign exchange stability, which must be respected by all member countries, to move back towards more fixed rates of exchange. One hopes that even the countries which have adopted flexible rates will increasingly follow three basic rules:
1. that their exchange rate policies should be publicly known;
2. that central bank intervention in the exchange markets is permissible and sometimes necessary;
3. that it is useful to tie each currency to a currency basket based on the country's trading relationships.

Basket currencies

The term 'basket currency' describes a new concept in the definition of national currencies. It is useful, but it is difficult to understand.

A basket of currencies (a basket currency) is a unit of account. Its purpose is to provide an unchanging numeraire or index with which particular national currencies can be compared or against which changes in their value can be judged. More than a quarter of the world's currencies are now pegged against a basket of currencies. The Special Drawing Right, consisting of known percentages of five major currencies, provides such a numeraire or index.

Another use of the basket idea is the daily exchange rate for sterling, quoted in the newspapers and described as the trade-weighted index. If it stands at 90.5%, this means that sterling is now worth 90.5% of what it was worth on average in 1975 (which is taken as 100). Rates for 18 currencies are included, in proportions appropriate to their share in UK trade in 1977. The dollar, for instance, accounts for 24.6% of the total and movements in the value of the dollar affect the trade-weighted index a great deal, but of course much less than the straightforward although less relevant sterling–dollar exchange rate. The statistical data are obtained from the Multilateral Exchange Rate Model of the International Monetary Fund.

Before February 1981 the date with which sterling was compared was not the average of 1975 but the rate on 18 December 1971, the date of the Smithsonian Settlement. The currencies included were different and had different weights, for example the dollar accounted for 32.8% instead of 24.6%. The trade flows used for the fixing of the index were those of 1972 and not those of 1977. It is clear that the change of index in 1981 invalidated comparisons: the pound was much weaker in 1975 than in 1971 so that the figure after February 1981, at about 100%, looked much better than the figure immediately before the change which stood at approximately 80%. There had in fact been no real change.

A similar basket concept is used for the US dollar and is also quoted in many newspapers.

The European Currency Unit (ECU) includes the currencies of the member countries of the European Community and is used extensively in the operation of the European Monetary System (EMS). Each currency accounts for an unchanging proportion of the ECU so that a change in the exchange rate of only one currency affects the international value of the ECU, but changes to different currencies included in the basket can, if in opposite directions and depending on their 'weight' within the basket, cancel out. The parity grid of cross-rates and the early warning system based on the 'divergence indicator' are seen in terms of ECUs.

Summary

There are aspects of basket currencies and trade-weighted indices which concern us all.

1. They are difficult to understand.
2. They give a more accurate picture of changes which occur than the old-fashioned comparison of the national currency with the currency of only one trading partner, for example the sterling–dollar rate alone or the dollar–Deutsche Mark rate alone.

In other fields we already accept this: a retail price index is more likely to tell us the true rate of inflation than the comparison of this year's price of one commodity, however widely consumed, with last year's price.

3. Changes in the base data invalidate comparisons. Using increasingly out-of-date base data also invalidates comparisons. This dilemma of the statistician is inevitable.

6
THE STERLING AREA

The sterling area was a currency area in the old-fashioned sense. The members of it kept their reserves in the currency of the area; they paid all foreign currency earnings into the currency reserves of the central country and in turn drew upon those reserves for their requirements of foreign currency. The United States is still such a currency area and for a long time the sterling area was of a similar kind. With the notable exception of Canada, it included most of the countries of the old British Empire, the present Commonwealth, and also one or two others.

This type of currency area presupposes a certain amount of political unity or at least a measure of central political control. It means that those who earn a great deal of foreign currency are willing to allow those who earn a great deal less to spend some of it.

A second meaning was added to the sterling area at the beginning of the Second World War when exchange control was first introduced. Under the Exchange Control Act 1947, which succeeded the wartime measures, payments from the United Kingdom to countries in the sterling area were not subject to exchange control, and therefore investments in those countries were entirely free. While it is true that a measure of voluntary restraint had been imposed at times upon payments from the United Kingdom to the so-called developed countries in the sterling area, namely Australia, New Zealand, South Africa and Eire, the general concept remained: exchange control affected payments by members of the sterling area to those outside it and the maintenance of assets outside the sterling area by residents of the sterling area. It did not interfere with payments within that area.

A currency area

When the British Empire was succeeded by the Commonwealth and the arrangement became progressively looser politically, the central administration of reserves ceased to have any real force. In so far as sterling area countries still kept their reserves in London, they did so under the set of guarantees known as the Basle agreements. The basic concept of these agreements (described in Chapter 9) was that member countries were entitled to diversify their reserves, that is, to convert them into a non-sterling-area currency whenever they wished, and further that some of the remainder of the balances held by them was guaranteed by Her Majesty's Government against any loss arising from a devaluation of the pound sterling. This guarantee by Her Majesty's Government was made possible by an undertaking on the part of 12 countries outside the sterling area to replace the sterling held by Commonwealth countries by their own increased holdings of that currency, should the countries of the sterling area at any point reduce their total holdings of sterling. In fact, such a guarantee had the effect of causing the sterling area countries not to reduce but to increase their holdings of sterling, which earned them a high rate of interest without any exchange risk. It does mean, however, that the concept of the sterling area as a true currency area ceased to have any real meaning. Whether it necessarily meant that sterling, as far as the Commonwealth was concerned, had to cease to be its reserve currency is an interesting subject for debate.

An exchange control area

However, the role of the sterling area as an exchange control unit remained, although this applied only to the United Kingdom itself. Other members of the sterling area did to a large extent impose exchange control measures on payments not only to those outside the sterling area, but also to those in other countries within it.

It can well be argued that the exchange control aspect of the sterling area had disadvantages and no commensurate advantages to the United Kingdom. Indeed, at times of economic crisis in the mid sixties the suggestion that the sterling area should be abolished, or in more technical language that the scheduled territories should be re-designated to include only the United Kingdom and not a large part of the Commonwealth, was under serious discussion.

This re-designation in fact took place in 1972, reducing the sterling area to contain only the United Kingdom, the Channel Islands, the Isle of Man, Eire and Gibraltar.

The United Kingdom balance of payments concerns payments to and receipts from any country outside the United Kingdom. The sterling area was treated for this purpose in exactly the same way as countries outside the sterling area, and payments to the old sterling area counted against the balance of payments just as much as payments outside. It was unreasonable to differentiate between the two types of payment, and to impose severe restrictions upon payments of a capital nature to the area outside the scheduled territories while placing no effective legal restrictions upon payments to the sterling area (and only a voluntary restraint upon payments to a small part of that area). A far greater degree of control should have been imposed at times of economic hardship by the British Government upon payments to the overseas sterling area as well as upon payments to the countries outside the sterling area.

After 1972 residents of the United Kingdom were prevented from paying monies to the so-called 'tax-havens' in the sterling area (except, of course, the Channel Islands and the Isle of Man which, for exchange control purposes, continued to count as part of the United Kingdom although they did not do so for purposes of taxation). In addition to controlling payments to tax-havens for investment, the imposition of exchange control between the United Kingdom and those tax-havens effectively prevented expatriation of resident funds from the United Kingdom to countries outside the sterling area through various well-known gaps. Some of these gaps were due to the strong position of certain countries inside the sterling area which made them unwilling to impose exchange control upon their own residents, although agreeing to operate exchange control upon funds emanating from the United Kingdom. Control in these cases was not wholly effective, although the total quantity of funds expatriated illegally by residents of the United Kingdom was fairly small.

The suspension of exchange control in 1979 put an end to the sterling area as an exchange control area. We can safely assume that the territory included in the sterling area or scheduled territories if exchange control is ever re-instated will be limited to the United Kingdom, the Channel Islands and the Isle of Man.

Summary

The large sterling area as a currency area and as an exchange control area is now a matter of the past. It was both a major contributory factor to the reserve currency role of sterling and an important aid to the performance of the pound in that capacity.

To have the national currency used as an international *reserve currency* has advantages and disadvantages. It provides a volume of foreign-owned monetary assets to supplement domestic resources and supports the country's financial institutions and economic activities. This is particularly true when the currency is the world's lead currency (as the dollar now is) or when the reserve function is part of fixed arrangements within certain territories (such as the sterling area or the French franc area used to provide). The disadvantages consist mainly in the volatility of funds and are most strongly felt and rightly feared when the currency is weak and there are no political ties which effectively restrict the movement of currency reserves from one home to another.

If sterling, even without its large sterling area, continues to perform a reserve function for other countries, this will be of benefit to the United Kingdom. It will also constitute danger and require vigilance and care in the control of money and the supervision over exchange rates.

7
THE EUROPEAN CURRENCY

The long-term aims of the European Community, as laid down in the Treaty of Rome 30 years ago, envisaged a growing similarity of economic standards and social conditions throughout Europe. This would eventually lead to exchange rates which, because economic conditions were no longer allowed to diverge, would not need to change one against the other. Alternatively, a single currency could then replace the separate currencies of Europe.

The Werner Plan

It is therefore not astonishing that, when in 1971 the governments of the then six Common Market countries made their reactions to the Werner Plan known, it became clear that the notion of a joint currency had to be taken seriously. The Plan was accepted.

The Werner Plan proposed increased co-operation between the central banks of the Common Market countries. In the initial years, the fluctuations between their currencies were to be reduced by a common policy of intervention in the foreign exchange market (the *snake*). Intervention against the US dollar was also to be a matter of joint policy and no longer a matter of individual national decisions (the *snake in the tunnel*).

Later – the Werner Plan said 1980 – the currencies of the member countries would be permanently and irrevocably tied to the existing exchange rates, then to remain unchanged for ever. This would mean neither fluctuations of exchange rates nor changes in parities thereafter.

To historians in the twenty-second century this will probably seem no more surprising than the unification of the Scottish and English currencies or the use of identical dollars throughout the United States seems to us. To us in the twentieth century such a change would be revolutionary, because we are conscious that sovereign states of considerable age are at the moment pursuing separate and even divergent economic policies and that, as long as they wish to do so, a joint and unified currency is impossible.

Tying together the European currencies would mean that no member of the European Community could devalue or revalue. This would give rise to two problems which merit careful consideration.

First, if no more exchange rate adjustments are possible, the agreement being irrevocable, then a few changes in parities will have to take place in the years before it becomes effective. Such changes would not be based just on past experience and the foreseeable future but also on a vague and uncertain assessment of longer-term economic, social and political developments.

Second, once the currencies are irrevocably tied to an existing exchange rate, devaluations and revaluations cease to be available as a remedy for economic difficulties. If, in addition, exchange control can no longer be exercised in normal times, the remaining possibilities for influencing the economic situation are all in the area of domestic economic and social policy. Deflationary measures will sooner or later be inevitable. The population which is suffering from a high inflation rate will have to accept unemployment, without unemployment benefits, or high taxation, or a wages and prices policy, or a credit squeeze and high interest rates. If it does not do so, the other members of the Community will have to support the ailing country indefinitely: foreign currency will have to be lent from a central fund to finance the country's excess spending. To idealists this may seem the ultimate in international charity, but it conjures up alarming possibilities in a world in which political democracy and the freedom of pressure groups to campaign for better conditions are both realities and sacred principles.

A short look at exchange rate fluctuations for the German mark, the pound or the French franc in the last 20 years suffices to illustrate the extent and duration of international aid which would have been needed had not exchange rate adjustments been possible as a last resort.

If the Werner Plan nevertheless becomes reality, one of the prerequisites – albeit an irksome one – for the establishment of a new reserve currency will have been created. This would on the one hand lighten the burden on the dollar and on the other reduce the benefits that the dollar derives from its role as lead currency. It would also mean that the European currencies might jointly carry the burden carried by sterling in the past. This is neither welcome nor appropriate.

The current reserve role of various European currencies is less important and less worrying than the immense responsibility for neighbouring economies which will burden the members of a fully developed Common Market. This is where the real difficulties of the next 10 years lie. Many problems still need to be solved for the economic and social development of Europe to be steady and positive. The involvement of as many nations as possible is just as important a part of this as the continuous development of a European sense of unity and neighbourly belonging together. Foreign exchange schemes cannot bring about such a development, but they certainly can and should support it.

The snake

The nickname, *the snake,* given to the currency arrangements in the initial stages of the Werner Plan arose from the visual presentation of the resulting rate pattern: when some currencies were near the top of the allowed band and some near the bottom, the snake was fat, when they were all bunched close together the snake was thin.

Between 1972 and 1976 Belgium and the Netherlands operated a smaller margin (1½%) than the others (2¼%) and thus created a smaller snake within the snake. This was known as *the worm*. The snake and worm are shown graphically in Figure 7.1.

The European currency 65

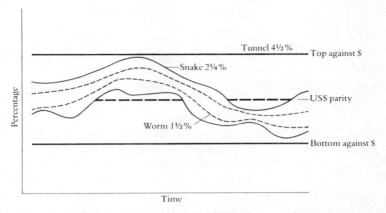

Figure 7.1. Graphical representation of the snake, the worm and the tunnel. Snake maximum = 2¼%, worm maximum = 1½%, tunnel maximum = 4½% (= 2¼% either side of parity).

The snake began its life in April 1972 and originally included Germany, Belgium, Holland, France and Italy. Participating central banks had to keep within 2¼% of the agreed middle rate. When the outer limits were reached the central banks of the two currencies involved had to trade the one against the other in the market place and thereby seek to counteract the prevailing trend. Swap arrangements between central banks provided them with the necessary foreign exchange to make such activity possible.

The United Kingdom joined in May 1972 and opted out of the arrangement in June. Denmark also took part from May until June 1972 and again from October 1972. Italy withdrew in February 1973 and France in January 1974. France came back in July 1975 and left again in March 1976. Sweden and Norway became snake members in March 1973 (Sweden until August 1977 and Norway until December 1978).

From 1972 until 1973 the European currencies had fixed rates against the US dollar so that they could only move against the dollar within a narrow band (2¼% either side of parity) and in unison. This gave rise to the term 'the snake in the tunnel'.

The European Monetary System

This, too, is a method for reducing short-term exchange rate movements between the participating currencies. It began operation in March 1979, as successor to the snake, and included Germany, Belgium, Holland, France, Italy, Denmark and Eire.

A central fund, the European Monetary Co-operation Fund, facilitates the settlement of payments resulting from intervention. Allowed margins are again 2¼% either side of parity, with an optional alternative (6%) available to facilitate the participation of countries liable to find their currencies under pressure.

Thanks partly to the determination of France and Germany to make the system work, the EMS survived its first 3 years with relatively few parity changes and with the general structure intact. Confidence in the survival of the EMS is growing.

The United Kingdom delayed its membership of the European Monetary System. It is not difficult to see that the commitment to less flexible exchange rates, which the EMS requires, places restraints on domestic economic policies. These would be outweighed by the assurance of more stable prices in trade with the other member countries. However, the main objections to British membership of the EMS are political.

Advantages and disadvantages

The financial and economic consequences of belonging to a currency area are complex and can vary dramatically from month to month. For this reason membership may be beneficial at one moment and detrimental at another. A balance needs to be struck to enable one to evaluate the likely effect over a longer period.

The main economic advantages of belonging to the EMS

1. Exchange rates are predictable and the exchange risks affecting imports from and exports to partner countries are limited.

The European currency

2. In so far as the system is seen to be taken seriously by the governments concerned and backed by sufficient resources, parity changes become both less frequent and less sudden. Speculation is less profitable and, as a result, less likely to occur and to distort seasonal and other predictable trends.
3. Internal and external influences on the exchange rate are shared by the currencies of partner countries and their impact is reduced, which may be welcome.
4. Internal and external influences on the exchange rates of partner countries have an impact on the exchange rate of the domestic currency and this may sometimes be welcome.
5. By belonging to a large currency block the effect of fluctuations in the exchange rates of non-member currencies (e.g. the US dollar) is shared by the country's main trading partners and joint policies to deal with them can be devised.

The main economic disadvantages of belonging to the EMS

1. When pressures become too great to resist, parity changes occur, the magnitude and timing of which are often hard to predict precisely.
2. Domestic economic policies, in particular those concerning the volume and cost of credit and those which directly affect the level of employment, are partly dependent upon the constraint of a fixed rate of exchange.
3. Internal and external influences on the exchange rate are shared by the currencies of partner countries and their impact is reduced, which may be unwelcome.
4. Internal and external influences on the exchange rates of partner countries have an impact on the exchange rate of the domestic currency and this may sometimes be unwelcome.
5. Central bank intervention results in an increase or a reduction in the domestic money supply and has to be counteracted by open-market operations or other measures.

No European reserve currency

Many European currencies are internationally strong and attract, because of this and because they are served by experienced financial institutions in their own financial centres, considerable business and large deposits from abroad. This ought not to encourage them to take the place of sterling as a reserve currency: that service is now performed by the dollar. In due course, the reserve role of national currencies must be taken over by a genuinely international currency developed from Special Drawing Rights. (This will be discussed in Chapter 9.)

8
GOLD

Gold has had monetary uses since time immemorial and its industrial uses were in earlier centuries closely linked to its monetary functions. Only in more recent times have these industrial uses been extended from jewellery to dentistry, electronics and others.

The history of gold

The most recent chapter in the story of gold as a reserve medium in the contemporary world starts in January 1934 when President Franklin D. Roosevelt raised the price of monetary gold to $35 per fine ounce. Several comparatively insignificant increases in the previous months had prepared the ground for this. His motives were to cause an inflation in raw material prices and thus to jerk the world out of the Great Depression.

The subsequent story has been overshadowed by the motives just referred to. It was difficult to accept that a rise in the price of monetary gold is inflationary only in certain circumstances, or that the price of monetary gold need not necessarily increase when world prices do so. Those who were exasperated with the unchanging price of monetary gold – still $35 per ounce in the 1960s – tended to point out that all other prices had doubled, trebled or quadrupled, and used this as an argument in favour of changing the price of monetary gold too.

The price of monetary gold is commercially relevant only when governments are free to use gold to increase their overseas expenditure and when they have no other way of doing so. With national currencies and Special Drawing

Rights now constituting half of the world's reserves[1] (and a proportion of every country's reserves), governments are no longer dependent on changes in the price of monetary gold for their increased expenditures overseas. The cry that the price of monetary gold is unrealistic has therefore long since ceased to be meaningful. Nor were the changes to $38 in December 1971 and to $42.20 in February 1973 of any real significance in this particular debate. The former was primarily necessitated by the need to find a politically acceptable formula for the revaluation of certain currencies such as those of Japan and France.

Different uses

Today, any consideration of the gold market must base itself firmly on the concept of the *two-tier system*. This was the arrangement made in the 1930s, operated until 1961 and re-introduced in 1968. It simply means that only central banks deal with each other at the official price and that all others meet in the world's markets and trade at a price reached freely by matching demand and supply. Provided international monetary discipline is effective, which it generally is, the two markets or tiers can be kept apart.

The operation of a two-tier system does mean, however, that high price levels in the free markets cause doubts as to whether the official price is not 'unrealistic' because it is much lower. This invariably encourages speculative gold-buying. This, in turn, raises the free market price and both inconveniences the genuine industrial users and rocks the international monetary boat. To obviate this the *Gold Pool* was formed in 1961.

[1] It is difficult to state the proportions precisely. Valued at the official price of $42.20 the monetary gold reserves amount to about 10% of the world's total gold and currency reserves. This is too modest a figure. If, however, these reserves are valued at the free market price (say $400) gold appears to constitute over half of the world's total gold and currency reserves. This is unrealistic as the bulk of the world's monetary gold can in practice not be sold, because it would swamp the market. There are over 30,000 tons of gold in government reserves; annual production is only around 1,000 tons.

Eight of the countries who were large holders of monetary gold agreed to feed a central Gold Pool in London in agreed proportions. This Pool was to supply gold at $35 per ounce to all buyers. It thus became unnecessary for industrial users or speculators to pay more than $35 for gold; the price on the free market dropped to this level. When this had been achieved, the activities of the Gold Pool were extended in 1962 to buying as well as selling gold at $35. As a result, the price could not drop below $35 an ounce and became in effect pegged at $35 for all purposes, whether monetary or commercial.

The Gold Pool's main justification was that it provided stable prices for the metal in the interests of industrial users and producers. This was even more important than in the case of other metals because of the unavoidable influence of speculative situations which were due to gold's monetary use. It also made the task of the Gold Pool more difficult: demand and supply might not alter radically or suddenly from ordinary commercial causes, but the second or monetary use of gold affected people's views at times of currency crises and tended to cause disproportionately large fluctuations in total demand.

Gold crises

During the months before and after the devaluation of sterling in 1967, gold-hoarding reached enormous proportions. Up to $4,000 million above the normal annual figure is said to have been spent that year on buying gold for this purpose. The eight Gold Pool countries had to give the gold to satisfy this extra demand and the gold content of the reserves of some of these countries thus dwindled rapidly. Italy and Belgium were rumoured to be short of gold. France disapproved of the idea of helping speculators by selling them gold on the basis of 'heads you win, tails you lose nothing' and left the Pool. The United States was at that time still bound by law to hold gold to an amount equivalent to 25% of its note circulation and was rapidly approaching that minimum level.[2]

[2] This rule was rescinded in March 1968.

All these facts pointed to the possibility of a change in the system. By the beginning of 1968, it was becoming apparent that the gold price would have to be raised or the one-tier Gold Pool system abandoned. In the event, the latter course was chosen on 17 March 1968. The world returned to the pre-1961 system, now called the two-tier system. Only governments dealing with monetary gold now had access to the United States Government at $35 and even they were asked not to buy. All others operated on the free market at a price dependent upon the state of the market. This was not ideal nor did it really suit the producers, but it was workable.

In August 1971 the United States formalized their unwillingness to sell gold even to central banks and terminated the link between the dollar and gold. The official price of monetary gold thus became as lacking in significance as the numerical size of a telephone number.

Demonetization in theory

The abolition of the official role of gold in the monetary system thus began in 1971. Some would claim that it has, at least in theory, been completed.

Amendments to the Articles of Agreement of the International Monetary Fund, which became effective in April 1978, had the objective of avoiding the meaningful re-establishment of a fixed price for gold. No longer do member countries subscribe to the fund partly in gold. No longer are exchange rates fixed or expressed in relationship to gold. No longer is the value of a Special Drawing Right defined in terms of gold. No longer are governments tied to an official price in their dealings with each other and in the market place.

Demonetization in practice

In practice demonetization has not gone very far. It is, of course, true that a slow phasing-out of gold from its official monetary role, if not necessarily from its function as a means of private hoarding, is bound to occur over the next few decades. Already its place in official monetary reserves has been reduced to only one-half of the total (see footnote on page 69) and this process seems destined to continue. To hasten the disuse of gold in monetary reserves beyond this present development would serve little useful purpose and create unnecessary difficulties.

The long-term trend of prices in the free gold market may again take gold up to $500 per ounce or beyond, which the producers would welcome in a period of rising costs of production, but this expectation is only reasonable insofar as the supply of gold and the industrial and hoarding uses of gold remain unchanged. A sudden unloading of a large part of present monetary gold stocks, sacked from their use as monetary reserves, would indubitably slash the free market price and ruin the gold-mining and refining industries in the Western world. For this reason, if for no other, the advocates of rapid demonetizing in practice need to be restrained. Sales of gold by the United States and by the International Monetary Fund since the 1978 changes in policy have been fairly substantial. They did not, however, cause a collapse in the free market price of gold because they coincided with a period of naturally rising prices due to industrial and speculative demand for gold.

Gold is still important both as a reserve asset for governments and as a store of value for individuals afraid of war or inflation. Its price should therefore be a matter of more active concern and it is desirable to establish an improved variant of the Gold Pool system of the sixties. While at times of heavy speculation the unconditional commitment by the major central banks to supply cheap gold to all and sundry became embarrassing and positively harmful to monetary stability, it is possible to visualize a system of regular official intervention in the free gold market which would counteract upward price trends from commercial causes without having also to be operated when the market is overwhelmed by speculative demand. Such a voluntary gold pool with the right to intervene or not, as its managers thought fit, would achieve steadier markets for producers and industrial consumers and reduce the extent to which the free market price of gold might otherwise rise or fall. If the gold price tends to rise such a system will help in the demonetizing process by drawing some gold stocks from monetary reserves to the free market.

Gold or paper money

The Industrial Revolution, followed by an unprecedented spread of knowledge and of technological know-how, has improved the material lot of mankind. They have also increased the world's population and confronted us with new and difficult problems in many fields, not least in that of economics. Unemployment and inflation haunt us as we prepare to banish poverty, malnutrition and sickness from the earth. We are still looking for a magic formula.

Surprisingly, some serious commentators have suggested that the magic can be found in a return to the gold standard. This was a simple system which limited a country's ability to spend overseas to the amount it could earn from foreigners plus its holding of gold. The gold reserves were usually rather small and not regarded as available for reckless shopping expeditions. The system thus acted as a discipline.

The gold reserves have now been replaced by larger reserves which include gold, the national currencies of other countries and substantial credit facilities including IMF Drawing Rights, Special Drawing Rights and central bank swaps. When cash runs short, borrowings take place. The government decides whether expenditure is necessary or avoidable, whether borrowing is sensible and constructive or irresponsible and unjustified.

The gold standard distributed reserves arbitrarily and provided a strait jacket. The more flexible reserve arrangements of the present time are related to the resources and requirements of the country in a much more realistic way. They can still seem like a strait jacket when times are difficult, but the possibility of temporary credit enables governments to face balance-of-payments problems. The discipline is no longer in the form of an arbitrary and inflexible stock of gold. This financial decision – when and how far to live on borrowed money – now depends largely on the courage of sophisticated ministers and ultimately on the good sense of those who vote for them. International bodies can provide general rules, give advice, impose penalties. The decision lies where the sovereignty lies, with those whose national currency it is.

Foreign currency reserves, like the domestic money supply, must not be inflated by the printing press or by easy credit. If they are, there must be good economic reasons, within carefully decided limits and for limited periods. The opportunities provided by the concept of paper money must be utilized with great restraint, if long-term disaster is not to follow the short-term improvement.

Prospects

Ever since the days of sun worship man has held gold in high esteem. (Indeed the notion of 12 silver coins equalling in value 1 gold coin is a formula harking back to the idea of 1 sun or gold year containing 12 moon or silver months.) As the violent story of mankind unfolded, this metal, then so rare and held therefore in almost religious esteem, became the one form of wealth which neither Biblical quotations nor hostile military action seemed able to destroy. Men stored their reserves in this form and it will take many decades yet before the last traces of this habit are lost. This is obviously less true in Anglo-Saxon countries where gold has been little held by private individuals than it is in France or the East where gold is still regarded as the best form of saving.

Modern scientific methods on the one hand and new forms of international financial collaboration on the other have provided us with adequate alternatives to gold as a reserve unit. There is, however, little evidence that mankind, especially in times of economic or political crisis, is as yet keen to substitute a different metal, a man-made substitute or paper money (whether national money like dollars or pounds, or international money like Special Drawing Rights) for the accustomed gold.

Recent events have thrown some doubt on accepted views about the free price of gold. Whereas in the past it had become normal to expect the price of gold to rise both at times of growing inflation (causing greater distrust of paper money) and at times of international tension (making people wish to hold a fairly mobile and easily recognized asset, which was independent of national government for its accepted value), there is some evidence to suggest that this is now less likely to happen.

It is impossible to differentiate accurately between speculation and hoarding or between hoarding and industrial uses. When is a gold bracelet an ornament and when is it an investment? When is a gold bust a piece of art and when is it a way of carrying a great amount of money across the world in times of war?

There is a possibility that the growing costs of storage and insurance will cause gold bullion, gold coins and golden jewellery to lose some of their attraction for hoarding purposes. Despite the political dangers of nationalization, land and house property are gaining in popularity as an alternative. The prices of other metals seem less volatile and more predictable precisely because their industrial uses are more important than their speculative and monetary ones. Even stocks and shares may become more widely sought as a store of value, as those in need of an inflation-proofed and revolution-safe nest-egg become more sophisticated and also more able to operate internationally.

Changes in hoarding habits and the continuing process of actual demonetization of gold may, over the next two decades, invalidate the dictum: because inflation is with us for ever the price of gold must continue to rise.

9
LIQUIDITY, RESERVES AND SPECIAL DRAWING RIGHTS

The *reserves* of a country are like the working capital of a company or the current account of an individual. In most countries they constitute the foreign currency balances of the central bank (about two thirds of which tend to be banked with other central banks and one third in the Eurocurrency market) and the gold held by the central bank, together with certain special items such as the newly created *Special Drawing Rights*. As with the cash balances held by individuals or companies, so also with the gold and currency reserves of countries, it is important to remember that they do not represent the total assets of those in whose name they stand. Indeed, some of the richest countries in the world have small foreign currency reserves, whereas some with very large foreign currency reserves have few other assets overseas. Such other assets might be in the form of stock exchange investments held by individual nationals, or subsidiaries owned by national companies in foreign countries. They also include such items as the currency balances of the commercial banks, which are of course part of the national reserve but not part of that more narrowly defined item, the *currency and gold reserves*.

What reserves are for

From time to time the currency and gold reserves will be needed for purchases of food and raw materials; at other times they will be replenished from the proceeds of goods which have been sold by residents to non-residents. There are periods in each year when countries spend money overseas which they will get back later; in the meantime they must have a fair amount of either cash or credit with which to make their purchases before the resulting earnings can be collected. It is for these purposes that reserves are held. How large these reserves need to be will depend on the type of trade of the particular country and on the type of pressures to which the country's currency is subject.

A country which imports raw materials and then earns foreign exchange, after a long period for manufacture and exportation, will need greater reserves than a purely agricultural country. A country whose currency is used for trade by other countries and in whose currency foreigners keep some of their reserves will, of course, be subject to greater fluctuations than others and will need greater currency and gold reserves. If there is any general key to the kind of reserves which a country ought to hold as working capital it is the old view that 50% or more of the previous year's importation bill is an appropriate amount of reserves to be held: anything less is insufficient, anything more is adequate. Since the oil price explosions of the seventies, however, such simple guide-lines have ceased to be appropriate.

It is quite clear that the reserves held by most countries have not risen as fast in the last 30 years as the money value of the goods in which they trade. The problem which this causes, namely a general shortage of liquidity the world over, has been discussed for a long time and in the mid sixties resulted in a decision by the International Monetary Fund to appoint a committee to investigate the matter. This committee was charged with finding ways to deal with the problem of the shortage of world liquidity and consisted of the Ministers of Finance of the 10 most industrialized countries in the world. Much of its work was done by a committee of the deputies of the Ministers of Finance under the chairmanship of Dr Otmar Emminger of Germany. The committee eventually reported its view on what should be done to increase the reserves held by various countries to make them more adequate at a time of growing international trade, and suggested the establishment of a new reserve medium which became known as Special Drawing Rights.

How Special Drawing Rights are used

When it was first decided to issue Special Drawing Rights, the intention was to do so to the extent of $1,000 million in each of the first 5 years, adding over 5 years some 8% to the total gold and currency reserves of the world, which were then standing at about $70,000 million. By the time sufficient countries had agreed to the establishment of Special Drawing Rights it was decided that the original issue should be on an increased scale: the first 3 years saw the issue of a total of $9,500 million of Special Drawing Rights. Of these, $3,500 million were issued on 1 January 1970, $3,000 million on 1 January 1971 and $3,000 million on 1 January 1972. At the beginning of 1979, 1980 and 1981 further Special Drawing Rights worth approximately US$4 billion each year were issued, bringing the total to about $21½ billion.

Special Drawing Rights are pieces of paper which are issued to each member of the International Monetary Fund and entitle that country to borrow from any other member a foreign currency needed for balance-of-payments purposes. Such borrowing is for a limited period and interest is payable. No member of the International Monetary Fund can be asked by other members to take in Special Drawing Rights as security for such currency borrowing beyond twice its own allotment of Special Drawing Rights.

The issue of Special Drawing Rights is made in proportion to the quota or shareholding in the International Monetary Fund. As this in turn is based upon each member's share in world trade, it follows that Special Drawing Rights are issued to countries in proportion to their share in world trade. This accords logically with the view that extra working capital was needed to enable countries to finance international trade, that is to say, to purchase goods abroad and pay for them before receiving the proceeds of exports.

When Special Drawing Rights were decided upon as the right way of alleviating the alleged shortage of world liquidity, it was intended to deal with a shortage of working capital rather than a shortage of money in the broader sense. Special Drawing Rights give countries the chance to spend on imports at times which are seasonally unfavourable to them. They do not enable them to increase over a long period their total importation in relation to total exportation. They do not help an underdeveloped country to make substantial capital investments which will need decades to repay. Indeed, Special Drawing Rights have been heavily criticized because they have not given any great advantage to the underdeveloped countries of the world. Such help as they have given has been to each country in proportion to its share in world trade: they have given much more help to the countries which are already rich than to the countries which are still poor. They were not primarily intended to deal with the needs of the Third World.

The future of world liquidity

The future of Special Drawing Rights is a matter for serious discussion among experts of every kind. It is probable that further issues of them will be made in increasing quantities in the years to come. Whether this will tend to support inflation will largely depend upon the monetary discipline imposed upon themselves by the governments of the countries which receive the largest amounts of Special Drawing Rights, these being mainly Japan, India, China, Australia and Saudi Arabia, the industrialized countries of Europe and North America, and the larger countries in Latin America.

Already Special Drawing Rights, which are frequently nick-named *paper gold,* have taken their place in reserves and constitute a proportion of the total monetary reserves of countries which belong to the IMF. They have caused the proportion held in monetary reserves in the Western world in the form of ordinary monetary gold to become less. This proportion will continue to alter in favour of currencies and Special Drawing Rights on the one hand and against monetary gold on the other. This means that, with the help of Special Drawing Rights, nothing stands in the way of the ultimate demonetizing of gold. No purpose would be served in rushing this process, but it is undoubtedly a process which has already begun and which cannot be completed without further issues of Special Drawing Rights.

Special Drawing Rights as numeraire

In the Guildhall in the City of London there are brass plates measuring 1 foot, 2 feet, 1 yard, 1 metre, 20 metres, 1 chain (66 feet) and 100 feet. These enable the public to compare other measurements with these standard units.

In a similar way, the international value of one unit of national money must be defined in terms of an easily ascertainable, unambiguous and generally known unit. This is known as the *numeraire*. In the past, silver or gold was used. Thus, from 1967 until 1971, the US dollar was equivalent to 0.88g of gold and the pound sterling to 2.11g, which gave an exchange rate of $2.40 = £1.00. The value of 1g of gold was fixed as arbitrarily as the brass lengths in the Guildhall (1 troy ounce or 31g = US$35). Gold was by common consent the numeraire.

As the dollar–gold relationship was fixed it was also possible to use the US dollar as the numeraire, and to define the value of other countries' currencies in terms of US dollars. This figure, which is made public and has legal and financial significance, is often called the parity or par value of the currency or, more recently and less formally, the central rate.[1]

The 1978 Amendment of the Statutes of the International Monetary Fund ruled that future definitions of this kind shall not use gold or a national currency as numeraire but a common denominator such as the Special Drawing Rights (see Schedule C Paragraph 1 of the amended Statutes). A number of countries have already defined the central value of their currencies in terms of Special Drawing Rights.

Special Drawing Rights as a world currency

Another aspect of Special Drawing Rights needs to be borne in mind. In 1968, a new version of the reserve role of sterling was established at the Basle meetings in July and September of that year. The Basle agreements consisted in fact of two

---

[1] This is not to be confused with the middle rate, which is simply the half-way point between the actual market buying rate and the actual market selling rate at a particular moment.

types of agreement. The first was between the United Kingdom Government and each of the governments of the sterling area. They fixed what proportion of those countries' sterling reserves could be turned into foreign currency and what proportion should be guaranteed by Her Majesty's Government against devaluation. This undertaking on the part of the United Kingdom would not have been possible, or at least would have been extremely imprudent, had it not been for the second set of agreements, between the United Kingdom Government and 12 countries outside the sterling area, by which those countries undertook to increase their holding of sterling if the sterling area countries reduced their holding of sterling below the level existing at the time of the agreement. It is interesting to speculate at what point in the history of monetary development this promise of the 12 countries outside the sterling area would have been replaced by a wider promise from all the countries of the International Monetary Fund to underwrite, and therefore in effect to take over, the obligations of the United Kingdom as the repository of the currency reserves of the sterling area countries. Such a funding of the sterling balances could well take the form of Special Drawing Rights, whether denominated in sterling and bearing a dollar guarantee or whether actually denominated in gold or in US dollars or representing their own independent value based on a basket of constituent currencies.

It is an interesting thought that Special Drawing Rights might thus have replaced the balances held in sterling by sterling area countries. This could well have been followed by the replacement of sterling balances held by other countries with Special Drawing Rights and later by the replacement of the dollar reserves held by so many countries with Special Drawing Rights. And, of course, as the money value of trade increased, further Special Drawing Rights would no doubt be issued, thus making the share of 'paper gold' in the total greatly exceed the share of real gold. Eventually this would lead to the complete demonetizing of monetary gold and the keeping of the currency reserves of all countries in Special Drawing Rights issued by the International Monetary Fund.

In one way, Special Drawing Rights, although *only an entitlement to credit* and not money in the strict sense, have the same use as money. Provided all those who are members of the International Monetary Fund accept the authority of the Fund and trust each other's promise to accept Special Drawing Rights as security for loans in national currency, there is no reason why Special Drawing Rights should not eventually replace all other reserves held by sovereign countries. They could also become the world currency of which the founding fathers of the International Monetary Fund were dreaming at Bretton Woods.

Such definition exists and provides the foundation for the eventual use of Special Drawing Rights as an international currency. The value of Special Drawing Rights is a composite or basket of the values of a number of national currencies in agreed proportions. Originally one Special Drawing Right equalled one US dollar. In 1974 it was valued in terms of a basket of 16 currencies. This was changed slightly in 1978 and more fundamentally at the beginning of 1981: since then the basket has contained only the currencies of the United States of America, France, Germany, Japan and the United Kingdom.

The final step in the progress of Special Drawing Rights to their acceptance as a world currency would consist in their replacing all national currencies and having a value defined without reference to any other currency and in fact replacing all other currencies in everybody's daily transactions. All over the world wages would be paid, vegetables bought, bets laid and prices quoted only in Special Drawing Rights.

It is unlikely that this will ever happen. It can be argued that it is not even desirable, as it would presuppose the complete abandoning of national sovereignty in the field of economics.

10
CURRENCY FREEDOM

In a free world, beset by a minimum of problems and blessed with a maximum of material prosperity, the right to acquire and keep foreign currency, and such assets abroad as it will buy, might be regarded as one of man's freedoms in the economic field. This chapter seeks to examine this concept and to show in which circumstances and to what extent this freedom ought to be limited, as of course in many countries it is and has to be.

Convertibility

Switzerland has been the country which has most consistently given to her residents the right to buy and hold assets of every kind situated outside her frontiers or denominated in foreign currencies. This amenity makes it possible for any holder of the domestic currency to demand and receive foreign currency at any time. Her currency can therefore be described as *fully convertible*.

Before any government can allow all holders of its national currency this liberty of conversion in any amount at any time for any purpose it is necessary for that government to be satisfied that the economy can support the consequences. In other words, the reserves of foreign exchange and the rate at which they grow must be sufficient to cover all such conversions with ease.

Undoubtedly Switzerland, by being able to remain neutral in the two great wars of this century, has succeeded in preserving and enhancing her currency reserves in a way which was beyond the reach of bigger countries with heavy international commitments. It is right to add that the Swiss have been helped by their wise use of natural resources, including the skill, knowledge and hard work of the population and of the foreigners who live and labour within the country.

Other countries, too, have been able to grant full convertibility of their national currency to their own citizens. The United States of America has always done so except for a period of limited restriction from 1968 until 1974 (the Foreign Direct Investment Program known as the Johnson Measures). Residents of the United Kingdom were given the right of full convertibility in 1979.

Full convertibility is, however, the exception rather than the rule. Many governments grant to their own residents only a limited form of convertibility, subject to detailed and inevitably irksome rules and regulations. This control over the acquisition and use of foreign exchange has been given the obvious name of *exchange control* and in the United Kingdom was governed by the Exchange Control Act 1947 until its suspension in 1979.

Why exchange control?

It is necessary to decide the circumstances in which this type of restriction on the economic freedom of residents may be justified.

There are three ways of increasing or at least preserving the national holding of foreign currency, most of which is held by or for the central bank and is shown in the published figures as the currency reserves of the country.

1. Foreign currency can be earned by goods sold, services rendered or inward investments received.
2. Foreign currency can be borrowed from foreign governments, international institutions or other sources.
3. Foreign currency can be obtained by selling overseas assets and long-term investments.

Of these three methods, the last two are often used, but are hardly desirable. They compare with the private individual's attempt to finance overspending by either borrowing from the bank or selling heirlooms. In most circumstances these are not solutions but stop-gaps. The proper course of action (though it is harsh to say so and even bank managers and rich aunts often shrink from putting this view too bluntly) is to spend less or work harder. In the international context, too, the temptation to live on capital or credit is hard to resist when these ways of countering a short-fall in foreign currency earnings are available. The relative ease with which governments can borrow abroad frequently delays the taking of harsh and necessary measures to improve the country's international earning power. Such delay hardly ever has any merit except in terms of party politics and even there it tends to backfire.

Once one accepts that the amounts of foreign currency earned and spent are the key to the long-term preservation of adequate currency reserves, the problem of how to control such transactions presents itself in earnest. The easiest and usually the most immediately effective way is to put direct controls on expenditure. This is why exchange control was originally introduced. It is certainly better than borrowing without prospect of repayment, but it is arguable that it is an improper way of dealing with this sort of trouble. It is like a medicine which brings down the temperature; it does not cure the patient. A case can even be made for the view that exchange control is a form of protectionism which sets up a defensive barrier behind which an inadequately productive or excessively expensive country can shelter.

Exchange control can only be avoided, in a country which is neither exceptionally rich nor unusually successful, if other steps are taken in good time to put the economy on the right road. Such measures may entail restricting wage claims and price increases by strict steps, which can include unemployment, punitive taxation, politically and socially painful cuts in government expenditure, and legislation affecting collective bargaining.

No government can view this kind of programme without distaste. The rate of inflation in countries with which its citizens either trade or compete will of course affect the extent to which it is necessary and the time it will take to become effective. It is neither surprising nor wrong to want to gain time by using the protectionism of exchange control to assist, to delay or even to avoid these measures.

Exchange control is, therefore, a mechanism which wise governments will be loath to dismantle completely. Those who advocate the complete removal of this tool (as would, for instance, result from the repeal of the Exchange Control Act 1947 in the United Kingdom) are allowing liberalism to move them from a very proper respect for economic freedom into a failure to appreciate the social consequences of allowing companies and individuals to dispose of national assets without restriction.

This is not to say that a reduction in the extent to which the acquisition and holding of foreign assets is controlled must not remain a proper object of governmental policy, especially when allied to a belief in economic liberty and the value of free markets. Politicians can keep and praise exchange control as a machine of government, but they should also make it known that its operation will be kept to a minimum at normal times. Long-term measures to put the economy on the right road are more important than short-term ways of avoiding the penalties which come from allowing it to stay indefinitely on the wrong one.

The future of exchange control

The United Kingdom controlled the purchase and use of foreign currency by residents from the outbreak of war in 1939 until the autumn of 1979. The Exchange Control Act 1947 replaced the Defence (Finance) Regulations 1939 and provided the parliamentary authority which the government needed to apply restrictions which were varied according to the economic situation and the tastes of the party in power.

In the United Kingdom the banks, whether British-owned or foreign-owned, acted as agents of the Bank of England. The Bank of England in turn carried out many of the functions which the Exchange Control Act granted to HM Treasury. The exchange control work of the banks was twofold: in many cases they studied and replied to requests by their customers under delegated powers laid down very clearly in the many Exchange Control Notices issued to them by the Bank of England from time to time. On the more unusual problems they merely advised their customers and passed the question to the Bank of England for decision, acting as go-between and advocate and putting their experience at the customer's disposal as part of their normal service. Indeed, exchange control could not have operated as smoothly as it did in the United Kingdom without the willing and expert co-operation of the whole banking community.

Although various arrangements to which the United Kingdom is a party (in particular the International Monetary Fund and the Organization for Economic Co-operation and Development) prohibited the imposing of restrictions on current payments, these were tolerated at times of severe balance-of-payments crises. The United Kingdom repeatedly imposed severe limitations on the use of currency for holiday travel abroad and for making charitable gifts to non-residents. This does not detract from the general theory that artificial controls on imports, foreign travel and so on serve, at best, a very temporary purpose. After a short while the advantage to the country imposing the controls is matched by a disadvantage to neighbouring countries who are forced in turn to restrict imports, foreign travel and so on, thus again worsening the original country's balance of payments. Controls on imports tend in the longer run to contract world trade rather than to improve the imposing country's balance of payments.

This effect is nothing like as certain where the controls are on transactions of a capital nature. Even those who see only disadvantages, to the restricting country and to the deprived recipients of her investments, have to concede that controls imposed upon the export of capital are an essential weapon in fighting adverse movements and are effective in curbing the activities of the more ruthless currency speculators at home.

In many countries which operate exchange control, so-called current payments are supervised rather than restricted. Imports may be paid for, services rendered by non-residents remunerated, gifts made, travel undertaken. Restrictions concern details: forward cover can be obtained for limited periods only and documentary evidence has to be produced for most transactions, to satisfy the bank handling the foreign exchange deal that a genuine and definite commercial transaction underlies the request for foreign currency.

Most industrialized countries, in accordance with Article VIII of the IMF Statutes, allow non-residents the right to convert holdings of national currency into foreign currency, but restrict similar action by resident companies or individuals.

Restrictions tend to affect mainly the purchase of securities denominated in foreign currency (*portfolio investment*), *direct investment* in industrial or commercial enterprises and the *acquisition of land* abroad.

New thinking

It is desirable to state clearly two aspects of exchange control which have only fairly recently been recognized as important and which may well affect political decisions about exchange control in the future.

First, exchange control has traditionally been a weapon to control outflows of money. Considerable changes in the currency reserves and therefore in the domestic money supply are however caused not only by outflows of money but also by inflows.

Inflows are harder to control because they are usually initiated by non-residents. The control of inflows is now part of the exchange control philosophy of many governments and has been attempted with a certain measure of success by surplus countries like Switzerland, Germany and Austria and even, for a short period in 1971, by the United Kingdom.

Second, the description earlier in this chapter of the Bank of England mechanism for the actual administration of exchange control draws attention to the fact that an efficient system requires a large staff in the offices of the appropriate ministries and of the central bank and also the intervention of thousands of well-trained staff in banking and industry. Such deployment of manpower on regulatory activities may well not be justified in terms of currency flows prevented by exchange control.

In times of heavy speculation ways are usually found to avoid the more irksome consequences of exchange control unless the regulations are exceedingly restrictive and their enforcement a great deal tighter than is generally found practicable nowadays.

Summary

The restrictions on currency convertibility which are the result of exchange control or similar systems can be of real help in protecting the currency reserves of a country and thereby in preventing, at least temporarily, undesired changes in the rate of exchange.

The danger is that exchange control will be used as a politically preferable alternative to more fundamental economic measures because it works swiftly and is inoffensive to the average voter. Indeed, spurious arguments alleging that the right to invest overseas may cause unemployment at home (when in all probability the alternative to overseas investment is not domestic investment but non-investment) illustrate the danger of ill-informed debates about this subject.

Nevertheless, for serious economic reasons as well as on political grounds, measures of exchange control, under this or another name, are bound to increase rather than diminish if financial markets remain free and trade grows. It is therefore necessary to know what exchange control can do to protect national currencies and when and how it should be used.

11
CAPITAL MOVEMENTS

Countries which have important financial and banking centres and whose currencies are widely used for international trade and investments are subject to large and sudden inward and outward movements of money. These may dwarf seasonal and longer-term changes in the balance of trade.

Special rates for money flows

One way of isolating capital flows and thereby insulating the price of goods, whether imported or exported, against unexpected and violent exchange rate fluctuations is to separate the exchange rate into two rates, one for current payments and the other for capital payments.

In the past this method has been used in France, Belgium and Italy. The *investment currency* of the United Kingdom, often referred to as the *investment dollar* or the *premium dollar* and giving rise to the famous *dollar premium* which affected overseas portfolio investment by UK residents for so many years, was another version of this dual currency system, although it operated only in one direction.

Arrangements of this kind are favoured by many financial experts but they are, strictly speaking, contrary to Section 3 of Article VIII of the Statutes of the International Monetary Fund and to the commitments accepted by the signatories of the Treaty of Rome concerning the free movement of capital at the official or commercial rate of exchange.

The pros and cons

Dual currency systems, which separate the allegedly non-vital payments and receipts of a financial kind from the essential payments and receipts on commercial or current account, were strongly defended by certain governments in Western Europe in the sixties and early seventies. They were seen as an answer to currency crises brought about mainly by large capital flows and deemed preferable to parity changes or the resorting to floating exchange rates or the increased use of exchange control. They were, in effect, intended to facilitate the fixing of the commercial exchange rate while allowing the financial exchange rate to float more or less freely.

In practice, dual exchange rate systems work well only when they are not really needed. When pressure builds up, the financial rate is only tenable for as long as the government keeps it artificially near the commercial rate, either by amending the rules or by direct quantitative intervention in the market.

The general philosophy, mentioned in Chapter 10, that current payments should not normally be restricted, whereas payments of a capital nature can legitimately be controlled in the interests of the currency reserves and the exchange rate, ought to be considered further. Is this distinction between commercial payments, deemed to be good in themselves, and capital payments, which are not necessarily evil but certainly prone to restrictions or price penalties as if they were mere national luxuries, a valid one? This question demands careful thought, lest we become the captives of facile generalizations. Two specific points may form a starting point for this contemplation.

1. Certain imports (e.g. of luxury goods like fashionwear or drink or exotic food or leisure equipment, or of articles which can be or are being produced in the home market although foreign makes are thought to be more fashionable, durable or efficient) are not more important for a hard-pressed economy than sensible capital expenditure. The latter will establish, support or develop suitable enterprises abroad which will bring steady and lasting returns to the domestic investor whether a manufacturing company, a pension fund or an individual.

2. The assumption, widely accepted since World War II and enshrined in so many international agreements, that trade is holy and investment a mere luxury, is often unjustified. Many countries would rather have another country's long-term investments, know-how and management skills added to their own endeavours to build a stronger industrial or agricultural economy than to receive comparable sums in payment for present goods and services and likely to leave no lasting benefit and often a further impetus to local inflation.

Lessons to be learned from the United Kingdom's investment currency

Until 1979 United Kingdom residents had to use *investment currency* for all purchases of quoted securities denominated in foreign currency. Special permission was also given for the use of this method for certain acquisitions of direct investments outside the sterling area, for the purchase of land and for investment in some mutual funds.

Investment currency was used for investment in any currency and in any country outside the sterling area. In fact, most of it was used for the purchase of securities denominated in US dollars and for this reason investment currency was often referred to as *investment dollars*.

The total investment currency available for use by residents of the United Kingdom varied from time to time, but it was not altered by changes in demand and supply. If demand and supply did not balance, the premium collected by the seller and paid by the buyer varied upwards if demand exceeded supply, and downwards if supply exceeded demand at that momemt. As only a small proportion of the total quantity of investment currency (the *investment currency pool* or the *investment dollar pool*) came on to the market at any one time, even fluctuations of several per cent in the premium did not really show a clear trend or express the views of the majority of holders of investment currency.

Influences on the rate

There were many reasons why the investment dollar was one of the most volatile and least predictable of currencies. Anyone wishing to purchase securities for which investment currency had to be used had to consider two distinct price trends. The highly skilled, professional investment managers who operated mostly in this field may have come to different conclusions at the same time, and their actual decisions will have been exceedingly hard to predict and will certainly have depended on highly individual and specialized considerations. Each time a decision regarding an overseas investment was made, two questions were asked and answered.

1. What do I expect the price of the share to be in x months' or years' time?
2. What do I expect the premium on investment currency to be at the end of the same period?

There were some simple influences which determined the answer to both questions. Good news from Wall Street alone was likely to suggest movement upwards in both cases, but good news from foreign *and* domestic industry could well suggest an upward movement in the case of question 1, but a downward one in question 2. This might make for a very difficult decision.

Summary

The British concept of investment currency was ingenious. It provided a large pool of foreign exchange for overseas investment by United Kingdom residents and enabled them to increase or reduce their holdings without directly affecting the UK currency reserves (although the 25% take-out rule which operated for some years forces one to qualify this statement).

The abolition of investment currency greatly simplified international investment activity. It also got rid of complex regulations leading to mistakes and inviting dishonesty. The effect on the reserves was not very great, partly because abolition coincided with growing trust in sterling as a petrocurrency and partly because the bigger investors had long since been allowed to invest abroad by other means, namely through the use of borrowed foreign currency.

Except for the professional dealer to whom the investment dollar offered excitement and opportunity, the demise of this financial dual rate and the amalgamation of the investment currency pool with the country's official reserves is no cause for regret. We need not fear its re-establishment, nor hope for it.

12
FOR OR AGAINST SPECULATORS

Who are the 'speculators'?

Few subjects connected with foreign exchange cause more discussion, inflame tempers more severely, or test the ingenuity of the accurate thinker or speaker more than does the term *'speculator'* and the idea of speculation. There are in fact two kinds of so-called speculators. Before we discuss whether speculation is always right or always wrong or, depending on the circumstances, sometimes right and sometimes wrong, we must try to differentiate between the two quite different kinds of people who are often described as speculators.

The true gambler

There are those who purchase a currency because they believe that it will increase in value, because of a seasonal trend or because of a long-term change in the rate, and who do so for no reason other than that they believe that they might sell again at a windfall profit. They do not need that currency and they will sell it as soon as it has appreciated sufficiently. If they are mistaken they will lose some money; if they are correct they will make quite a lot. This kind of speculation is like buying a share for a quick profit, like backing a horse in a race, like buying a property with no intention of living in it but because one believes that a change in planning permissions will increase the value of the land quite out of proportion in a very short period of time. It is essentially the action of a man who buys something which he does not need to use. Equally, it may be the action of a man who sells something he has not got for future delivery with the hope of buying it back substantially more cheaply before the date of delivery arrives; again, if he is mistaken he will have to buy in at a loss, but if he is right he will make a handsome profit.

This kind of speculator is the grand speculator; he is rare, he has to be clever to be successful and he has to be rich to dare to operate in substantial amounts. For all these reasons it is unlikely that he is the kind of speculator who will seriously endanger a currency or disturb a government, although ministers tend to talk about him as if he were the biggest threat to the national currency and to the stability of the national economy.

The careful insurer

The much more common speculator is not the man who buys a currency because he believes it will appreciate or sells a currency because he believes it will depreciate, but the man who must, by the nature of his business, be it in trade or investment, hold or receive foreign currencies. To him it is not a desire that the value of currencies in relation to his own currency should change, but a threat, a fear, a danger overhanging his every action. He protects himself as best he can when he hears rumours or suggestions of a change of rate which might affect his business adversely: he will sell at the earliest possible moment a currency which is under pressure or buy at the earliest possible moment a currency which is deemed capable of revaluation.

When this is done by a large number of people in many countries it is described as the phenomenon of *leads and lags:* one group leads or goes ahead of the normal time-sequence and the other lags behind or delays. When this occurs, no permanent damage is done to the national currency which is under pressure, but a temporary outflow of reserves will result. If those who are buying foreign currency are doing so several months sooner than usual, whereas those who are selling it are doing so several months later than usual, this temporarily depletes the reserves and can add to the troubles of the government. It is this kind of activity, born not of an urge to make a quick penny but of a desire to protect one's own business with all the legal means at one's disposal, which is often described as speculative. It is in fact purely protective, but can in moments of crisis be of a size to put real pressure on, and therefore present a true danger to, the stability of the national currency.

Whose side are you on?

It is therefore important in discussing both the effect and the morality of speculators to keep apart these two entirely different types of action: the one designed to protect legitimately the business being done by the commercial and investing community; the other, much more rare, much less substantial in size, much more open to doubt by moralists or politicians, which is out merely to make profits. Often speeches or articles which castigate speculation and which blame speculators for the downfall of a currency try to ascribe to the rarer gambler the effects which are, in fact, the result of the legitimate action of the trader or banker protecting by legal means his proper commercial interests. The worst that can be said of such protective action is that it will accelerate the moment of danger which may or may not lead to a new rate of exchange.

The true gambling speculator is rare; it is arguable that his action is not in the national interest. It is much more difficult to find convincing reasons for saying that his action is immoral. He is doing with money what other people do with shares, land and other forms of investment. He is buying what he believes will appreciate and selling what he believes will get cheaper. Nor is it always easy to draw a clear line between the gambling speculator and the protective merchant, for even the very rich international operator who buys and sells currencies purely for profit will, when challenged, reply that he is in fact protecting the value of his capital and the resulting income with which he does whatever he has chosen to do, good or bad. So even if we believed that the pure speculator was an evil man, we might yet find it difficult to discover an actual instance of this rare but much-discussed individual. He is presumably the 'Gnome of Zurich' so dear to government spokesmen. He can be blamed for the effects of their own economic mismanagement. His replies are unlikely to be heard.

Role of the speculator

Let us then accept that the real speculators are rare; that those to whom we usually refer as speculators are, in fact, not true speculators and that the result of their action, if sufficiently massive, is likely to accelerate a change rather than to cause it. Should we necessarily view the action of all types of operators, speculative or protective, as being undesirable? We have lived through many currency crises in recent years which have tended to give us the impression that speculative movements in the international currency field are disturbing, upsetting, unsettling, undesirable and to be avoided. At times they have led to a breakdown in the forward market, at others they have necessitated the actual closing of all foreign exchange markets to the great detriment and worry of those who had legitimate business to transact. Undoubtedly, such extreme crises occur relatively rarely, although we had to live through a number of them in close succession during the years of transition from strictly fixed parities to managed floating.

The action of the speculator is likely to occur on three different levels of intensity. There is, first of all, the action of the true speculator operating in an undistinguished and unsung fashion as a foreign exchange dealer of a banking house, who buys from a customer or sells to a customer a currency which that customer wishes to trade but which the banker cannot immediately cover in the foreign exchange market. In deciding to trade at a rate acceptable to the customer he is taking up a speculative position in that currency by pitting his own judgement about the future trend in price against all the vicissitudes of the market-place. He is a true speculator and no foreign exchange dealer doing this humdrum kind of transaction day by day and hour by hour at the behest of his customers would be ashamed to admit to being a speculator by profession. His action may not shake the currencies of the world, but it assuredly helps to make the wheels of trade turn. Without it the market would be a less effective place for his customers; prices would be less favourable and at times it would be impossible to conclude deals merely because a commercial counterpart is not available. A professional foreign exchange dealer in the bank interposes himself in such a situation by making a speculative judgement and taking speculative action. This is not only the least dangerous but also the most desirable form of speculation. It goes on all the time.

The second kind of speculation occurs when the image of a national currency is beginning to attract the attention of economists, journalists, commentators and bankers, so that people will either buy it or sell it in the expectation of a change. The resulting pressure on the demand–supply relationship, and therefore on the price of that currency, may be the first public intimation that something is amiss. The action of the speculator, be he the gambling type or the protecting type of our previous distinction, may well give the first indication of an underlying illness. In this case, the speculators are causing a fever which is the signal of a disease; the foreign exchange market is acting as a thermometer to indicate that the patient is in ill health. This function of the speculator is surely a healthy one and if heeded in good time can be of real assistance to statesmen and economists in assessing the underlying aspects of the economic situation.

It is only when such a situation has got out of hand and far beyond the need of a thermometer, when the patient is not just slightly feverish but plainly in dire distress, that the speculator hastens the onset of crisis. It is only in those rare situations when every other indication and signal, every other warning and comment has been ignored and the situation is almost out of hand that the speculator's function, whether commercially legitimate or not, can be regarded as entirely undesirable from the national point of view. That still does not mean that the speculator should be outlawed and forbidden to act. Indeed, countries which prohibit the legitimate covering of forward commitments to their importers at times when the national currency is under pressure, while stopping a real drain on their currency resources, are attacking one of the proper rights of the commercial community. Even when speculation is against the national interest it certainly should not be forbidden.

Much speculation, as we have already seen, is the result of the legitimate protection of the interests of an individual or a company in an economic situation which, through no fault of that individual or company, has become a danger to his normal trading or investing activities. In such a situation speculation can undoubtedly be disturbing to the government, but the action of the speculator is in no sense reprehensible or immoral or to be banned by legal measures. To speculate is to take a view about the future. To forbid speculation is to forbid commercial activity.

Governments versus speculation

The fact that speculation is an activity which at times is beneficial to the market and, therefore, to the market's customers is not to say that it does not at other times cause considerable danger and distress to those in charge of the national currency, namely the government. It is, therefore, not surprising that governments should take steps to counteract or lessen the effects of substantial speculation. This has been organized in an increasing way in recent decades, partly through the framework of the International Monetary Fund and partly through other steps within smaller groups of countries, often under the general supervision of the International Monetary Fund, the Bank for International Settlements or the authorities of the European Monetary System. Governments can borrow foreign currency in substantial amounts when their own currency is under pressure, and their own currency reserves are therefore dwindling, from countries who are in a more fortunate position. Indeed, these steps were used so frequently during the crises of the mid sixties that the idea was mooted of making such help almost automatic, and the name *automatic recycling* was actually given to the scheme, never implemented, which some people advocated to make this kind of aid available as soon as speculative flows of money occurred.

While one welcomes the availability of substantial international aid for countries which are either temporarily gaining or temporarily losing massive quantities of foreign exchange, it is undesirable that this aid should be wholly automatic. It is unreasonable that lenders should be called upon to lend, without limit on the quantity or the time of the loan, to countries which are in trouble. It is also unreasonable that countries should be able to receive amounts of money of this magnitude irrespective of other people's judgement as to whether such help is in fact the best way of dealing with the situation. Both lenders and borrowers must be entitled to examine on each occasion whether an adjustment in the rate of exchange or drastic internal measures would not be more appropriate steps for dealing with the causes of the speculative flow of money than their mere neutralization by automatic recycling. Nevertheless, moving funds from the country which has gained reserves to the country which has lost them has now become an exercise in international co-operation as swift and as substantial as it is ever likely to be, and indeed as swift and as substantial as it ought to be if the warning signal which speculation provides to those in power is not to be entirely lost.

13
THE CAUSES OF CURRENCY CRISES AND THEIR CURE

The system of floating exchange rates on the one hand and the enormous growth of the Eurocurrency markets on the other have made it easier than ever before to delay appropriate domestic action to restore the balance of payments. As a result currency crises can now often be delayed and the steps to cure them postponed. This chapter tries to throw some light on the difficult and far-reaching decisions which governments need to take and on the principles they might follow when they or their neighbours are facing exchange rate problems.

To tell or not to tell

There is little doubt that the consequences of currency crises are severe, although it may well be said that the cure is often more troublesome than the ailment. It is undoubtedly unpleasant to hear that the reserves of a country are dwindling, that the balance of payments is in substantial and permanent deficit and that 'something needs to be done'. This trend may well continue for a long time without being detected by the population at large, provided nobody in authority draws attention to the state of affairs.

Attempts to cure the situation involve painful and severe economic measures. Dealing with the currency crisis requires the attention and indeed the collaboration of the whole population.

There have been periods of severe but unseen disturbance for the balance of payments, such as occurred in the United Kingdom immediately before the 1964 General Election when, in the absence of governmental comment, the population as a whole was unaware of the seriousness of the situation. On the other hand, there have been times, such as in the United Kingdom in the years between 1964 and 1967, when comment caused people to believe that the crisis was even worse than it actually was. Often this very process of enlightening the population about the trouble which has already arisen adds a climate of fearful anticipation and speculation which aggravates the underlying situation rather than resolves it.

No solution is possible in a democratic country unless such a climate of opinion exists, but the feeling is no solution in itself. The belief that the balance of payments is bad leads to gloom, to a flight of capital from the country and to all kinds of consequences which are in themselves harmful rather than beneficial; yet without such an atmosphere the political and economic measures required to achieve a cure are very unlikely to be introduced by the government or accepted by the nation.

It is one of the undeniable penalties of democratic freedom that an understanding of the economic situation by the population at large is a precondition of the government's successful action in improving the situation. For it is the nation, rather than the government, that bears the consequences of the severe measures without which a currency crisis cannot be overcome.

Causes of currency crises

A currency crisis can be caused in two ways: it can have an external origin or an organic one.

External troubles

Certain currency crises are caused by pressures from outside which have no direct connection with the economic situation in the country concerned and which cannot be cured by measures taken by that country's government, although of course they can be effectively counteracted. One thinks, for instance, of the severe pressure against the pound sterling in the summer of 1969; this, at a time of a strengthening economic situation in the United Kingdom with a decline in the speculation against the pound, was due entirely to the movement into the German mark, which was deemed to be ripe for revaluation and indeed was revalued that autumn. The purchase of German marks put great pressure upon less fortunate currencies, such as the US dollar and the pound sterling, and the pound moved very close to its lowest point at 2.38. This was a crisis caused by external factors and was in fact observed without great alarm by the authorities in the United Kingdom and the financiers and bankers in the City of London. The pound was allowed to decline in the certain expectation that once the German crisis was over the pound would also recover. And so indeed it did.

There are many instances of this kind of action upon a national currency, sometimes caused by events in other countries or pressures surrounding other currencies, sometimes caused by speculation concerning the future price of gold or political events elsewhere which result in large shifts of money across frontiers. Their effect, if long-lasting, can be detrimental to the currency, but the permanent cure lies outside the control of that government acting on its own.

Organic weakness

Currency crises of organic origin cannot be cured by measures taken by foreign governments and present the gravest problems.

The modern international monetary system has provided us with a number of arrangements, some automatic, some subject to relatively quick confirmation in the case of need, which enable a government to borrow additional foreign currency, or to lend it if embarrassed by an excess of such currency, to counteract flows of money, whether speculative or commercial, into or out of the currency reserves. These measures, appropriate in a situation in which the interaction of national economies in international trade and the importance of world prosperity is recognized, should not blind us to the fact that a currency crisis caused by an economic situation in a particular country ought to be dealt with not by palliatives provided by international organizations or wealthier neighbours, but by the resolute action of the country concerned. More specifically, action needs to be taken by the people of that country, guided, and if need be compelled, by that country's government.

Currency crises of this kind are caused in a very simple way, although their recognition may be both delayed and disputed. They are caused by persistent overspending of the foreign currency reserves of the country.

As with an individual or a family or a company, a country cannot spend more than it earns unless it has a substantial amount of accumulated capital. Such cases are relatively rare, but they do exist. The United States of America consciously and indeed deliberately spent more than it earned abroad for many years after the Second World War, thus reducing its accumulated currency reserves in an attempt to give money to other nations of the world who required it not only for recovery, but in order to become the necessary export market for American manufactured goods. This action by the United States was, of course, wise and indeed at one time necessary for the economic well-being of the world; but it was made possible only by the enormous accumulated reserves of the United States. The situation has altered now; it exists even less in other countries where the currency and gold reserves, which are the spare cash kept for shopping expeditions in the future, are in most cases considered to be barely adequate.

If one accepts the traditional view that it is necessary for a country to hold in gold and foreign exchange as reserves at least 50% of the annual import bill, then an examination of the gold and currency reserves of most industrialized countries today reveals that very few of them have adequate backing. Even where there are such reserves, these dwindle very quickly if month after month and year after year the nation spends abroad more than foreigners spend in their country.

Currency reserves are simply the accumulated profit from international trade, investment and other transactions. Whether the earnings are due to exports or to services rendered to foreigners or are the income from past investment, the truth of the matter is that the balance of payments must be in surplus or positive if those reserves are to increase. If the balance of payments is in overall deficit, the reserves will diminish. In most cases, this process of diminution cannot go on for many months before the total size of the reserves appears wholly inadequate to serve the purpose for which they are intended. The critical size of a country's reserves is a matter of opinion rather than of scientific fact. A substantial change in the reserves in either direction tends to cause comment. Countries which have very large reserves regard themselves as on the verge of bankruptcy when their reserves are reduced to a smaller figure, even though that figure would seem excessively large to some of their neighbours. Because there is no clear standard for the necessary size of national reserves, it is dangerous for any nation to tolerate substantial and persistent decreases or increases in the country's gold and currency reserves without taking action to redress the balance.

Difficulties of avoidance

A persistent decline in the currency reserves caused by an imbalance in the trade figures calls for severe measures to reduce inflation, through steps to deflate the economy by economic or financial or fiscal means. Where the form of government is democratic, and in particular where an election is imminent, it is almost impossible for a government to persuade the population to accept measures which may involve such unpleasant legislation as increasing taxation, raising the rate of interest or forbidding wage increases, price rises or the distribution of unlimited dividends, unless it can first violently, strongly, persuasively and usually protractedly, lecture to the population on the causes, the extent and the necessary cure for the crisis which already exists. It is this delay in a democracy between the decline in the balance of payments and the enforcement by government of necessarily stringent countermeasures which can lead to a crisis of such magnitude that it can only be dealt with by a major upheaval like devaluation, or by a policy of deflation far more harsh and prolonged than would have been necessary had steps been taken at the earliest sign of trouble.

It can be argued that currency crises caused not by uncontrollable external factors but by an organic economic situation at home cannot at present be dealt with quickly enough in a democratically governed country. If this is so, then considerable thought ought to be given to the problem.

The nation must accept that a permanent deficit in the balance of payments puts unbearable pressure on the gold and currency reserves and therefore leads inevitably to a crisis and on to a painful cure. We must find ways in which this situation can be made less painful. The population must be made aware by clearer and more intelligible statistics, and by plainer and more honest explanations by those in authority, when a situation builds up which will require adjustment or reversal and which will get out of hand if such adjustment or reversal is delayed too long. It must become recognized as the duty of a government to give a warning and not to delay this for political motives until the situation has become a great deal worse.

In recent years there has been a tendency by politicians (not only in the United Kingdom but in several of the major countries of North America and the European continent) to avoid some of the more severe economic warnings at times when the party in power could not afford to make political mistakes. The fallacy in this situation is not that politicians are keen to win elections and anxious not to disappoint their would-be voters just before the elections take place. This is normal and natural. Rather, the fallacy is that governments have increasingly spoken as if they were the masters of the economic situation, not merely adjusting here and there by fiscal and financial methods what was taking place in the nation, but in some grand and almost superhuman manner shaping the economy of the country. It is merely a fantasy flattering to politicians and a convenient way by which the man in the street can shift blame for economic disasters and difficulties on to 'them'.

It is the work, the output and the productivity of millions of people in each country which make, or do not make, sufficient goods to keep their country prosperous, and it is the desire for pleasure, for leisure and for consumer goods on the part of millions of people which causes inflationary pressures in any particular country at any particular time. Inflation is the reduction in the domestic value or purchasing power of money which occurs when more is being spent when more is not also being produced. It is true that, in a highly centralized and planned modern society, the government can exert a certain amount of influence and control, but it is plainly false to expect the government to do everything single-handed and to accept blame, or indeed claim credit, for the economic situation.

It is only when we recognize that it is not the government which makes a country rich or poor but the people, by the work they do and the way they spend their money, that we shall cease to make the economic necessities of the nation subservient to political arguments at election time. Of course, economic policy is important and at times overwhelmingly important in the whole field of political activity, but in this, almost more than in any other aspect of government, the politicians are dependent upon the people and the intentions of the people in forming, shaping and guiding the economic destiny of their country. It is this recognition which will enable us to meet the difficulties and dangers in the economic situation and to allow governments to guide, warn and lead the economic endeavour of the nation as a whole without fear of parliamentary defeat or electoral disaster. Otherwise, as political freedom increases in democracies, we are bound to fall more frequently and more deeply into the economic crises which have in recent years tended to nullify, and at times almost to destroy, the political strength of those nations.

Disadvantages of persistent surplus

It is a little more difficult at first sight to understand why excessive currency reserves, the result of a persistent and substantial balance-of-payments surplus over a number of months or years, should cause any embarrassment at all.

There are two reasons why currency reserves above a certain level, which have resulted from a persistent surplus in the balance of payments, are undesirable. First of all, there is no doubt that the arrival of large amounts of foreign currency in a country causes a series of transactions which, if unchecked, have detrimental effects on the economy. The exporter who receives foreign money which neither he nor another trader needs for the purchase of imports, and which therefore becomes part of the surplus of the balance of payments, turns the foreign currency into his own currency by doing a foreign exchange deal with his bank. The bank, in turn, finding purchasers of foreign currency are scarce (that is what we mean by a surplus in the balance of payments), has to sell that foreign currency to the central bank of the country. The central bank adds this foreign currency to its currency reserves, thus showing an increase in the reserves when the figures are next published, usually at the end of the month. This, however, is not the end of the story, because the central bank has paid for this by giving its own domestic currency in exchange. A surplus in the balance of payments is matched by an increase in the circulation of domestic money, unless special steps are taken by the central bank.

The Canadian Government, for instance, made it known after they had changed the parity of their currency by the device of allowing it to float upwards in 1970, that one of their reasons for so doing was the difficulty of preventing the Canadian dollar equivalent of foreign currency from being added to the circulation of money in Canada, thereby accelerating the process of inflation. The story of the successive surpluses on the German balance of payments and the long years of struggle to deal with that, culminating in the revaluations of 1961 and 1969 and the decisions to 'float' upwards in 1971 and 1973, is evidence of the same problem. In other words, a substantial and persistent surplus on the balance of payments is likely to have inflationary effects.

There is a second difficulty. The total reserves of the world do not change except by unusual devices such as the issue of Special Drawing Rights. If any country has a surplus on the balance of payments, some other country or countries must have a deficit. If the reserves of one country increase, then the reserves of other countries must decline. The country in surplus cannot idly watch its neighbours labouring under persistent deficit, because its neighbours are, after all, its customers also and the surplus is due to its success in selling to them. If that success exceeds certain limits, the governments of these neighbouring countries will inevitably have to take measures, whether of deflation or devaluation, to make the excess of imports over exports less marked. This means that the country in surplus will find its own excess of exports over imports reduced by such measures.

A persistent and substantial surplus must therefore be viewed not only as possibly detrimental to the domestic economic situation, but also as a warning signal that the international balance of trade is in a situation which will rapidly become intolerable to the trading partners of the surplus country, and which it, as much as they, must help to redress.

Steps to be taken

Governments usually consider three types of measures when imbalances in the terms of trade, or one-way capital flows, threaten to cause a substantial or persistent deficit or surplus in the balance of payments. These measures can be taken either before a crisis develops and before speculation adds its weight to the existing and underlying trends, or as soon after the occurrence of such a crisis as is politically possible.

Short-term borrowing

Moves can be made with the help of international organizations, such as the International Monetary Fund and the Bank for International Settlements, or individual countries with substantial currency reserves, to give temporary aid in the form of loans for short periods or of currency swaps to the countries whose currencies are under pressure.

Such measures will not only give adequate funds to the country concerned, but also assure everybody that international help is available on a substantial scale. This alone may suffice to restore belief that not only the government concerned but its allies too will stand by the present exchange rate and will do all they can to undertake and support the economic measures necessary to put things right.

Public relations

A second measure, linked with the foregoing, is to assure all concerned that the situation has been recognized as being in need of adjustment, that the necessary steps have been examined and decided upon and that they will be taken resolutely and irrespective of the political consequences.

This is not as easy an undertaking as it may sound, as the history of the last 30 years has proved. It is difficult in practice because so often the people addressed are not the people who ought to be addressed. Often politicians are warned by their advisers of the dangers in terms which do not impress the politicians but frighten the traders who are at the heart of the situation. Sometimes the language is appropriate to the businessman when the banker should be spoken to, or appropriate to the banker when the statesman in a foreign country is the one actually listening to the speech.

The governments of the world (with few, rare exceptions) are unfortunate in their efforts to calm the waters when the tempests rage. Rarely are their statements as reassuring as they intend or wish. It is not easy to propose a solution. Politicians might often be well advised to consult the foreign exchange traders and some of their industrial customers before making statements designed to reduce speculative pressures. They would quickly be told that what they intend saying might cause greater fright and suspicion, while carrying little conviction.

It is one of the basic beliefs of foreign exchange dealers, and of traders in any commodity, that the best way to stop a speculator selling is to appear as a substantial buyer oneself. No words which tell the fellow that he is mistaken, stupid or immoral are anything like as effective as the action of the man who actually goes out to buy when the general trend is to sell. This approach is so basic to the philosophy of the market-place that it is a matter of endless amazement to foreign exchange dealers that politicians feel it best at moments of crisis to make speeches telling the world that the situation is hopeless but that there is no need for panic.

In the process of telling the electorate that the situation is serious and that action needs to be taken, they frequently convince traders that the situation of the currency is desperate. Why be surprised then if speculation, instead of ending, breaks out with renewed vigour? The public relations of managing a currency are a field to which little attention has as yet been paid, but which is crucial at times of pressure or of crisis.

Economic reforms

When international aid of a short-term nature has been given and an improvement in the general climate of opinion through word and action has been achieved, there still remains the removal of the basic situation of imbalance: the need to cure the crisis by removing the causes of it and to bring back into balance the balance of payments. It may even be necessary (particularly if the situation has deteriorated over a long period) not merely to halt but actually to reverse the trend, so that the losses already made may be put right within a period of relatively few months or years.

There is no easy way of doing this. An imbalance in the balance of payments is due to an underlying trend in the movement of money, the origins of which are deeply rooted in the country's economy and the effects of which have probably developed with accelerating speed over a fairly long period. The usual situation is that a rate of inflation greater than that in neighbouring countries has resulted in a deficit or a rate of inflation less than that in neighbouring countries in a surplus in the balance of payments. Such trends, being the result of prices and wages and every aspect of the cost of living, cannot be reversed or even made to change direction overnight. It is much easier to restrain such developments than to reverse them after they have occurred.

In the short run, inflation may not cause a deficit on the balance of payments, but eventually it is bound to do so unless other countries with which trade is carried on have similarly high rates of inflation. This is not to say that inflation is harmless if it is indulged in by all countries. The relevant point here is that its harmful effects will not include a balance-of-payments crisis.

Controls and restrictions

Direct controls on the movement of money between one country and another (such as import quotas, import deposits, exchange control restrictions on the movement of capital, and many others) can improve the balance of payments, and therefore counteract the effect of inflation on the balance of payments. It is important to recognize that different regulations, particularly in the field of exchange control, operating in different countries, will give unequal advantages to different countries by cushioning the effect of their domestic economic situation in terms of the balance of payments and the currency reserves.

It is true that exchange control is one of the methods which can most quickly and effectively deal with the balance-of-payments effects of run-away inflation (at least for a period). However, the long-term disadvantages of excessive exchange control measures are undoubtedly too serious to be wholly ignored in a community which depends not only upon industrial production, but also upon the free operation of the financial market-place for its prosperity.

Prevention of currency crises

As with any other illness, although there are now many known cures for a balance-of-payments crisis, the longer the patient is allowed to ignore the illness and delay taking action to deal with it, the more difficult it is for the doctor to apply the necessary remedies effectively, efficiently and quickly without at the same time doing real damage to the patient's metabolism.

Some of the tragic stories of lack of industrial growth and of persistent unemployment are the result of deflationary measures taken too late to deal with balance-of-payments crises in highly industrialized countries. The ideal answer is for complex modern societies to see to it that they watch the effects of domestic economic measures on the balance of payments much more closely, and that they take measures to put matters right at the very earliest signs of damage being done to the value and stability of the currency. Only harm is likely to come from any delay due to mere hope for an improvement in the domestic situation or a worsening in that of neighbouring states; resolute action must be taken while relatively minor measures of restraint can still have sufficient results.

The tragedy of the long struggle against revaluation in Germany and the long struggle against devaluation in Britain in the mid sixties ought to remain as warnings for all time against hoping instead of acting, and against relying on temporary measures such as international recycling of speculative funds, IMF loans, swap agreements between central banks, and so on, when a long-term solution applied at once is the right answer.

As is sometimes the case in the field of modern medicine, the international financial expert is all too easily tempted to rely on using the improved quantity and quality of available medicines to deal with severe economic ills, when these could well have been avoided by early diagnosis and early action. Economies can deteriorate into economic ill-health far more easily than they could before the Second World War because the availability of international aid makes the immediate consequences less catastrophic.

Summary

A currency crisis is precipitated when the balance of payments is persistently in surplus or in deficit for a number of months or even years, as a result of which the currency reserves of the country have: (*a*) dwindled to a level deemed to be inadequate in the light of the country's normal trading activities and in comparison with the amount of currency reserves to which people have become accustomed in the case of that particular country; or (*b*) increased to such a level that they are out of proportion to the normal needs of that country. Most people have no difficulty in understanding the problems which result from inadequate currency reserves because these difficulties are so similar to those of an individual whose bank account is nearly running dry, or of a company which has inadequate cash resources to carry on its normal trading activities.

The best cure for currency crises is for all governments to take economic measures at the earliest signs of an imbalance in the payments position, thus avoiding currency crises altogether. It must be one's hope that in due course more and more potential currency crises will not need the brilliant intervention of international financiers of all nations, but will be avoided altogether by preventive national action being taken in good time. Currency crises start in one country; they should be dealt with there before they spread.

14
EURODOLLARS

The *Eurodollar* marks a new development which has profoundly influenced the money and capital markets of the western world. For the first time in history we have moved from the concept of the financial centre serving people living outside the national frontiers, as London and New York did in the past, to one of an international centre which serves the world and has no one city or country as its focal point. The Eurodollar concept is the beginning of a truly international and even supranational market, although it still uses a national currency as the vehicle for its operations. The money and capital market in currency which belongs to no single country and is expressed in a unit of account such as Special Drawing Rights or European Currency Units is still in its infancy.

Eurodollars are dollars which are borrowed by banking institutions outside the United States[1] from banks or other firms outside the United States. Some of the borrowers are overseas branches of Amercian banks who are now among the most important participants in this market. Others are banks anywhere outside the dollar area: they may be in Europe, Asia, Canada or South America for instance, although, as the name of the Eurodollar implies, the initiators of this movement in the 1950s were banks in Europe, mostly in London. When the borrowing or lending is done by a bank in South East Asia or the Far East the Eurodollars are usually called *Asian dollars* instead.

There are two ways of calculating how many Eurodollars are in existence at any one time. The second way is the one normally used.

[1]This must now include the International Banking Facilities in the United States.

The lenders of Eurodollars are mostly industrial firms or central banks with accumulations of US dollars on their bank accounts in New York which for the moment they wish neither to spend nor to sell. They therefore put them on deposit or loan them to the reputable bank which pays them the highest rate of interest. If the borrower is outside the United States, the lending is regarded as a Eurodollar transaction. It is true, however, that no banker borrows money except to lend it to a user of money; if the money is the national currency of the United States, then the ultimate user must be buying something American. Indeed, the borrower will not take the loan or pay interest until the day on which he or his borrower or the ultimate borrower has to make the payment in US dollars to someone in the United States. If, therefore, Eurodollars are defined as US dollars which are borrowed by a banking institution outside the United States, these dollars, on this view, will cease to be Eurodollars on the same day, because they are usually spent in the United States on the day on which a bank outside the United States borrows and lends them. By nightfall they have reverted to being ordinary US dollars put by an American company into its account with an American bank. There are no Eurodollars in existence at the end of each working day. There are merely dollars.

The other way of counting Eurodollars is to include all former Eurodollars, whatever they have been used for in the meantime, until the borrowing bank outside the United States has repaid them to the industrial firm or bank of origin. By taking into account all outstanding loans in this way, the Eurocurrency total becomes very impressive and has in a quarter of a century soared from modest beginnings to well over $1,000,000 million, of which approximately 70% is actually in US dollars.

Origins of the Eurodollar

Eurodollars came into existence because of Regulation Q issued by the Board of Governors of the US Federal Reserve System, which forbade the paying of interest to depositors above a certain level lower than the banks would otherwise have been willing to concede. On the other hand, the prime rate assured American banks a return on money which was higher than necessary in the case of first-class borrowers. European banks were prepared to pay more and charge less, thus cutting the bankers' profit margin; the Eurodollar market, a free money market in US dollars outside the United States, was born. Other factors then greatly contributed to its phenomenal growth. Soviet unwillingness in the early sixties to deposit large amounts of money in New York in their own name was one of them.

Even the complete abolition of Regulation Q and of the agreed minimum charge for lending at prime rate in the United States would not now spell the end of the Eurodollar market. The convenience of a supranational money market and the development of the appropriate institutional expertise would seem to ensure that this market will not be disbanded, unless of course governments combine for political or macro-economic reasons to forbid citizens access to and participation in any money or capital market beyond strictly national boundaries.

Uses of the Eurodollar

The uses of Eurodollars, and to a lesser extent of other Eurocurrencies, are varied and changing. Listing some of the chief types of transaction is not likely to give a complete picture of either the past or the possible future of this market, but it should serve to illustrate the ways in which the market can be used, provided certain general conditions continue to exist.

These general conditions seem to fall into two groups. The first group is to do with exchange control. Many Eurocurrency transactions, as we shall see, are only undertaken because those wishing to borrow are prevented from doing so at home and in their own currency by limitations imposed under some exchange control regulation of their own government. Others are free to borrow but find that in the natural place for such borrowing the banks and other lenders are barred, again by some type of exchange control regulation, from lending for some purposes or to certain classes of borrowers. One of the commonest controls imposed in defence of weak reserves is to prevent the lending of the national currency by residents to non-residents. This often includes lending by resident banks to local subsidiaries of foreign companies.

The second group of conditions has to do with interest rates. In many countries, banking institutions are protected against excessive undercutting, either by mutual agreement or by legal enactments controlling interest rates. Whether these limit interest payable, stipulate a minimum level for interest charged, or do both, their effect is to make any institution not subject to these rules able to select certain transactions and to finance them at rates more favourable to the customer and less profitable to themselves. If the transactions selected are those with little risk and if the business is an addition to, rather than instead of, the institution's normal activities, the lower profit margin is acceptable. Institutions most likely to be able to profit in this way are banks in another country.

Not all restrictions upon interest rates are intended merely to protect domestic banks. Many countries impose such rules to affect the level of credit, the inflow of foreign money or the flight of domestic capital. Some of these could perhaps be controlled by more direct prohibitions of the kind associated with exchange control; others could not. In any event, countries with little or no exchange control prefer steps which directly (by government order) or indirectly (as by the imposition of reserve requirements for certain classes of deposits) determine interest rates. By so doing, they furnish inadvertently the preconditions for a Eurocurrency market in their currencies; and in so far as such a market flourishes, it weakens the effectiveness of the government's controlling measures. Eurocurrency transactions move the borrowing business from the national financial centres to a foreign place; they do not move the national money, which continues to be banked and spent in its own country.

Development of the Eurodollar market

Original customers of the Eurodollar market were firms in Europe and the Far East which found Eurodollars a cheaper way of financing their imports from the United States, and from other areas which demanded payment in US dollars, than borrowing US dollars in New York or their own currency from their own bank. Often the borrower was not the actual industrial user, but his local banker whose reputation and international standing not only helped to obtain a lower rate of interest, but also made sure that lending limits fixed by the lending banks remained sufficient to accommodate growing demand from certain countries and certain industries. Later the Eurocurrency markets were inflated by a variety of new developments, some of which need to be described here. It is an interesting exercise, important as it is difficult, to decide how far new uses of the Eurodollar market are the result or the cause of its growth.

For many years, the authorities in the United Kingdom encouraged the use of Eurocurrencies for overseas direct investments, because the UK reserves were growing at an insufficient pace to allow funds from the currency reserves to be allocated for this purpose. By financing projects through overseas borrowing, whether in local currency or in Eurocurrencies, industrial companies were able to proceed immediately with profitable investments. In most cases the company obtained credit as cheaply as, or even more cheaply than, at home, but took an exchange risk for the whole period of the borrowing. On balance this was much better for most companies than being refused permission altogether, and was possibly almost as attractive as being allowed to remit funds from the United Kingdom at the official rate of exchange. The justification for the arrangement lay in the advantage to the country, which thereby avoided a debit to the currency reserves that would only have been reversed, although perhaps a thousandfold, in years to come: this would be a good thing for the country in the long run, but no real consolation to the Chancellor of the Exchequer at the time the investment was first made.

This call on the Eurocurrency market by UK companies indubitably drove Eurocurrency rates upwards and therefore helped to attract funds which would otherwise have been invested locally in the United States. This cause of the growth of the Eurodollar market was the more substantial because the authorities in the United Kingdom added other categories over the years. Not only were those seeking direct investments outside the sterling area increasingly forced to finance them through a Eurodollar borrowing, but UK companies wishing to make direct investments in the sterling area, foreign companies wishing to make direct investments in the United Kingdom, certain British companies wishing to purchase foreign shares, and even some British institutions and companies wanting to make new investments in the United Kingdom at times of a credit restriction, were forced to borrow foreign currencies to do so. This put upward pressure on interest rates for Eurodollars and other Eurocurrencies. In turn, this attracted lenders of money to these supranational markets.

Very similar effects were felt when the United States took steps in January 1968 to control the outflow of funds for direct investment overseas, measures which remained in force until early 1974. Overseas subsidiaries of US companies, finding it in many cases hard to obtain credit from local sources, turned increasingly to the Eurodollar market.

At the same time, measures in the United States resulted in a shortage of money at home which led many American banks to compete for Eurodollar funds through their own overseas offices. This process of repatriation was the first real link between two competing markets, the Eurodollar market and the New York market, and showed that the use of a national currency for a supranational market inevitably complicates the operation of national economic measures designed to deal with a domestic situation. On the other hand, it is foolish to exaggerate this difficulty, because the funds in the Eurodollar market are in any case banked in the United States. The movement of funds from a non-American firm, via a European office of an American bank, to the domestic customer in the United States does not by itself increase the amount of credit available in the United States. If this sum were banked directly with a bank in the United States, the effect would be the same.

The growing experience of banking institutions in Europe contributed to the development of the Eurobond market, a supranational market for raising long-term capital for use anywhere in the world. This development was made possible by the rapid growth of the Eurodollar market in the 1960s. It depends to some extent on the ability of some houses to borrow short and lend long, which presupposes a pool of money which is both large and stable.

The future

The willingness, which developed over the years, of international institutions and central banks to lend to commercial banks active in the Eurocurrency markets some of their dollar reserves, instead of leaving them with the Federal Reserve Bank, has added greatly to the supply of Eurodollars. It has kept Eurodollar interest rates lower than they would otherwise have been, and has added substantially to the size and constructively to the sophistication and stability of this market. It has also enabled central banks (as became apparent in the pre-revaluation crisis in Germany in 1969) to counteract and influence movements in domestic interest rates and in exchange rates which occur when speculation is on an unusually large scale.

A market which has reached a certain age and a certain size ceases to be a phenomenon of a particular decade and develops efficient and mature institutions. Such developments as the Dollar Certificates of Deposit with a good secondary market, and the establishment of international Eurocurrency brokers who bring together borrowers and lenders in different countries, have added to the institutional framework which supports this relatively new money and capital market.

To some extent the foregoing remarks answer the questions, which are so often asked, of whether the Eurodollar is to remain part of the international monetary scene and what will be its long-term role and significance. No one single change, such as the abolition of exchange control in a major country or the removal of all American restrictions in the banking field, would now suffice to destroy the Eurodollar market. Nor is it easy to visualize the United States alone taking steps which could make the functioning of an overseas market denominated in US dollars impossible, although such measures are theoretically feasible. If, for instance, payments between non-resident banks and others which cannot be shown to be straight foreign exchange deals were subjected to a severe handling charge by banks in the United States, this might make Eurodollar deals uncompetitive. However, it would make institutions seek other Eurocurrencies as an alternative rather than return to old-fashioned financing in New York. Such measures, even if technically and politically feasible, would need to be taken simultaneously by all major countries if they were to be effective in destroying the supranational money markets.

The other way of restricting these markets is for individual governments to prohibit access to supranational markets by their own residents. If done in unison by many major countries, this would certainly restrict the size and therefore the usefulnesss of supranational markets. It is unlikely that governments would take this step unless the supranational markets could be shown to be internationally harmful or dangerous. In the absence of such evidence, governments are unlikely to place restrictions on access to these markets because it is generally in their own interests: it enables their own residents to do a variety of useful and profitable things which the country's balance-of-payments position makes it impossible to do with their own accumulated reserves of foreign exchange. If anyone is worse off, it is the country whose currency is being borrowed or the country in whose territory the project is being developed, not the country whose nationals are being enabled to proceed by this method. Furthermore, the substantial share which the commercial banks have taken in the recycling of the so-called petrodollars since the mid seventies, while not universally approved of, is seen by many as a beneficial way of using the expert knowledge of the banking community in the pursuit of global financing activities.

Dangers

What then are the international dangers which might one day unite the financial authorities of many countries in deciding to destroy or restrict this supranational money market? In fact, many of the weaknesses of the Eurodollar market are more in the nature of teething troubles than of organic hazards. Because many loans are arranged by dealers on the telephone or telex there is a risk of lending, often without security, to companies in a foreign country without a full examination of credit-worthiness and the complete knowledge of a business derived from years of personal contact between banker and customer. Lending limits are of course fixed in each bank, but unavoidably, where overseas firms are under consideration, only some of the bank's officers are fully conversant with the information which is taken into account in fixing them. Nor is there any way of knowing whether a borrower has also taken Eurodollar loans from other lenders, adding up to total short-term repayment commitments which are far beyond his means. Whereas a bank can in many countries find out fairly easily its domestic customers' financial arrangements, this becomes impossible where the customer is abroad, new and fairly large.

It is true that a loss made by a lender of Eurocurrencies as the result of the borrower's inability to repay will also be a loss of currency reserves to the lender's country and therefore a matter of serious concern to its central bank. But these situations are being increasingly avoided as bankers, in the light of past experience both of pre-war overseas lending and of Eurocurrency loans, establish practices which assure to Eurocurrency business the same care and safety as is usual in domestic banking. In highly competitive market conditions this is not always easy; the interests of shareholders and the country coincide in making such care essential.

A different type of problem confronts us when the possible cause of default is not the inability of a specific borrower to repay, but the shortage of currency available to the country in which the borrower is situated. Whether the borrower is the government itself or a state-owned industry, or an industrial or financial entity in the private sector, such difficulties have become a frequent and serious threat to international banking in recent years. Both the assessment of these 'sovereign risks' and the proper way of dealing with them have rightly become matters of grave concern.

Other disadvantages of a supranational money market are connected with the degree of independence from national measures of economic control which those participating in such a market are bound to enjoy. There is no reason to begrudge the professionals in the banking world their ability to earn money by giving a service to non-residents and thereby to collect foreign exchange. It is only when the authorities allow overseas borrowing for domestic projects that there is a net loss of foreign exchange, because residents owe interest to non-residents. When the authorities do not think this can be justified, they do not allow it: they maintain or establish exchange control to prevent such borrowing beyond a reasonable measure.

The real problems come from the extent to which domestic measures of economic control can be frustrated by the use of the national currency by those outside that control. Often this is compensated by the advantage, already mentioned, which the use of the supranational market offers to the same country. But is this enough? Has not the Eurodollar made it at times more difficult to control the availability of money in the United States, or Eurosterling more difficult to combat speculation against the pound? The Eurocurrencies are not additional money outside the countries concerned, but merely some of that money. The liberty of Eurocurrencies is not in the field of money supply, but of the use of credit. The impossibility of directing non-resident banks regarding the parties to whom and the purposes for which money is to be lent does weaken governmental control over its currency if it has a share in the Eurocurrency market. We must therefore expect occasional attempts at control, which can be effective only if they are made jointly by a number of the countries involved.

If, however, there ever were to be a supranational or world currency, the weakening of national economic policies would come from the nature of this currency rather than from activities in the supranational money or capital markets.

In the meantime, governments will continue to express more doubts about the advantages of Eurocurrency markets than are normally heard from industry. And yet some hestitation ought to be felt by the financial managers of industrial companies before they embark on Eurocurrency transactions. Indeed, many of them devote much time and thought to these difficulties already.

Risks to industry

It is often true that a Eurocurrency borrowing makes possible the financing at a reasonable rate of interest of a transaction which either a general squeeze on credit or specific controls concerning overseas expenditure would otherwise make impossible. It is tempting in such circumstances to clutch at a straw without examining its real strength.

There is in Eurocurrency borrowing a disadvantage, apart from the usual problems such as the viability of the project financed, which may have to be accepted but must never be ignored by the industrial or commercial borrower of Eurocurrencies. This is the risk of a change in the exchange rate.

Repayment of loans will normally come out of the earnings of the project and, more rarely and unhappily, from the general funds of the parent company. It follows, therefore, that the exchange risk lies in the possibility of the borrowed currency being upvalued (after it has been received and before it is repaid) in comparison with the currency in which earnings are expected, or with the currency in which the short-fall of earnings will be paid from central reserves. Equally, a devaluation of the currency to be received against the currency owed, during the period of the loan, will entail an extra cost to the borrower.

The difficulty of assessing the extent of this risk is far

greater than the difficulty of honestly admitting its theoretical existence. Each case presents its own special aspects. A general answer can merely point to the most common facets of the problem.

It may not always be easy to predict with any degree of accuracy the extent of the earnings of a new venture during the loan period, nor what exact proportions can be expected in each of a number of currencies. Much will depend on the relative ability of sales forces and on economic conditions and import controls in the various countries where sales are being attempted.

Even if precise receipts in each of a number of currencies could be worked out, nobody can be expected to predict accurately over a period of 5 or 7 years whether an adverse change in the exchange rate is merely a possibility or rather a probability. Nor would the knowledge of a probable or certain change during the loan period help in taking the decision whether to borrow or not, unless the amount of the change can be predicted. Where a 25% devaluation might kill a scheme, a 10% devaluation is often irksome but bearable.

In general terms, two rules of thumb can guide one in taking the decision, although by themselves they are insufficient to lead infallibly to the right decision.

1. The period of the loan is often decisive in assessing whether to accept the inevitable exchange risk. An exchange loss of 10% is not compensated by a saving of 2% per annum on interest on a 3-year loan, but it would be on a borrowing for a 10-year period. Tax rules need, of course, to be taken into account too.
2. The other important consideration is a factual and careful comparison of the proposed loan with alternative ways of borrowing. The case where one is considering an alternative which is only different in that it costs slightly more in interest is quite different from the all-too-common situation where exchange control or the exigencies of the money market present the scrapping or indefinite postponement of the project as the only real alternative. In such cases, a rather high

exchange risk may have to be accepted if the project is believed to be really profitable.

In most cases the exchange risks, whether deemed large or small, bearable or unbearable, cannot be covered by insurance. The forward market rarely offers long enough periods and is in any event usually too costly for this type of capital operation. In countries where absence of alternative methods rather than cheapness sends borrowers to the Eurocurrency markets, there is normally also a rule which forbids the purchase of the necessary cover on a forward basis.

Only companies with wide international ramifications can hope to avoid the inevitable exchange risk of Eurocurrency operations, but this does not in practice exclude smaller organizations from this relatively new market: Eurocurrencies involve risks, which are, however, often outweighed by the advantages and opportunities offered.

15
FORECASTING EXCHANGE RATES

This chapter aims to answer some of the questions of principle which deeply concern the businessman, especially when a system of largely floating exchange rates is in operation.

Why?

Exchange rates can move against each other by 10% or 20% in a year. They can also move by that amount and return to the original figure within a few weeks. The second development is much harder to predict than the first. It also constitutes a much greater risk because the decision about the exact timing of a foreign exchange deal can, as a consequence of almost arbitrary short-term fluctuations, double or obliterate the commercial profit on one's own transaction or on that of one's competitor.

One of the results of the change from fairly fixed exchange rates to largely floating exchange rates in the seventies has been the need to obtain help in predicting both long-term trends and violent short-term fluctuations in the comparative values of national currencies.

Forecasting has become big business. At its best, it is of real help to the troubled operator. At its worst, it is an expensive exercise in trying to know the unknowable. We need to know in advance in which direction an exchange rate will move, by how much, and when.

How?

There are two common approaches to forecasting exchange rates. They are usually utilized in conjunction with one another, which is good. Unfortunately, they are often expressed in highly technical, very specialized and frequently mathematical language.

The approach that appears at first sight to be the less scientific, sometimes called qualitative, looks at such factors as the trade balance, the money supply situation and its likely effect on inflation and employment. It also considers the currency reserves and changes in their size, overseas assets and overseas debts, the level of investment and the need for modernization or change in industry, the strictness of and the politically possible changes to exchange control, and the world economic situation and its likely impact on domestic production and consumption. Short-term flows of capital, government philosophy, electoral prospects, market feelings, interest rates and land prices and wage rates, social and economic pressures, the age and ability of management in industry and in banking, and the efficiency and effect of trade union structures are also taken into account.

When you have looked carefully and calmly at all these and at some other factors, you can hazard a guess at the likely changes in the value of the national currency, and at the likely extent and likely timing of such changes.

The other method, associated with charts and models and largely dependent on the use of computers, is often called econometric. An initial decision as to which of the economic indicators to include in the model and what weight to attach to them is essential. By now most forecasters accept that this method can only work if it also takes into account the political and psychological factors which play so great and often so unpredictable a part both in the decisions of governments and in the reactions of markets.

The fundamental ingredient in any currency forecast is gut feeling, which is really the gift of judgement. It is partly intellectual and partly intuitive. It is partly congenital and partly acquired. It belongs to people rather than organizations and explains why the successes in the market place are achieved by individuals or by well-led teams and not necessarily by well-equipped companies.

Whatever method or combination of methods is used to forecast exchange rates, one fundamental fact must never be forgotten: an exchange rate requires a comparison between *two* national currencies. Any evaluation of the situation, and of trends affecting the situation favourably or adversely, must take into account the essentially comparative nature of exchange rates. We are not looking at an objective value, nor comparing today with yesterday, but comparing today here with today over there, and tomorrow here with tomorrow over there.

When?

By the time fundamental developments of an economic and political kind have begun to be written about in newspapers and in specialized periodicals, markets may react by buying and selling in expectation of the consequent price changes. Alternatively, they might ignore the suggested developments and thereby express scepticism of the viewpoint the media are presenting. In either event, the market's reaction to the reports gives helpful indications to the businessman. It is, however, too late for genuine forecasting.

Forecasting needs to be done and evaluated and, if this is appropriate, acted upon before the information and its likely effect on the market are publicly known.

In practice, companies exposed or likely to become exposed to exchange risks must make it a rule to obtain and to consider views about likely exchange rate changes as soon as a commercial project is discussed. The conclusion reached must be backed by knowledge and judgement. Optimism must be restrained by the need for caution. Forecasts must be recognized as possibly fallible, rather in the realm of prophecy than in the arena of certainty. Above all, studies must be updated, decisions reviewed, and conclusions sometimes courageously revised from time to time.

Summary

Forecasting exchange rates is necessary and impossible. The good prophet is rare and worth listening to. The best forecaster is more aware of the difficulty of his task than of his remarkable achievements in the past. He remembers that foreign exchange is part science and part art. He is most useful to his client when he remembers that factual knowledge and sensitive intuition are the true ingredients of successful activity in the market place.

16

CHARTING A COURSE THROUGH TURBULENT SEAS

We look for simple indicators which will enable us to compare the economic performance of various currency areas and help us to predict movements in exchange rates. The wish is perfectly reasonable even though we know it to be impossible to fulfil.

Because we seek straightforward, intelligible, uncomplicated theories to aid us in our task of foreseeing currency developments, we fall prey to popular theories. These tend to reign for a year or two and are then replaced by a different theory. This chapter examines briefly some of these theories.

Most of the theories are not in themselves valid as explanations of exchange rate movements in the past or as guides for the correct assessment of likely trends. Their validity, such as it is, lies in the support which is given to them during the height of their popularity. This support may start among academics, from whom it spreads to journalists, who owe it to their readers to explain events plausibly and simply. The impact of the media is such as to persuade the exchange dealers and their customers to accept the validity of a simple and clear doctrine, which appears to explain the past and to predict the future: at best it is correct, at worst it is respectable; if it leads you astray you will lose money, but you will not lose your job.

One other aspect of these theories is important. If paramount importance is attached to certain indicators at a particular period, then the pointers which these indicators give will be believed and will be acted upon. The effect of this is that, at least in the short-run, the rates will do for commercial reasons what the indicators predicted on theoretical grounds. The prophecies become conveniently self-fulfilling. The vulgar way of putting this is in the form of a question: how many people have to be wrong to make them right?

In foreign exchange there is obvious danger in getting on the bandwagon. Sometimes it is even riskier to refuse to do so.

Inflation rates as indicators

The oldest of the popular theories in the field is the Purchasing Power Parity Theory of Money. It suggests that differential rates of inflation in different countries will eventually lead to a compensating adjustment in the rates of exchange. Under a floating rate system this adjustment will happen continuously; under a fixed rate system it will happen at intervals and take the form of a big change of parity (devaluation or revaluation).

Statistics can be found to prove or disprove the validity of this theory. That it has some validity is undeniable: a country with price increases 5% higher than those in neighbouring countries each year for 4 consecutive years will find its goods about 20% more expensive in world markets than those of its competitors and will be unlikely to maintain its share in world trade unless it devalues its currency by about 20%. This is delightfully simple but is it true?

The quality and speciality of its exports, the geographical location of the country and of its markets, the proportion of its products which are exported, the importance of imports for local consumption, the initial level of costs and the impact of altered profits on industrial or agricultural activity, these and many more will decide whether the Purchasing Power Parity Theory in its simple and pure form is applicable.

It is certain that it does not explain many of the biggest exchange rate movements of this century and even more certain that, taken by itself, it is a poor guide for exchange rate prediction.

The effect of interest rates on exchange rates

For many decades it was usual to regard currencies which were borrowed and lent at high rates of interest with suspicion and to try and sell them. Conversely, currencies whose interest rates were low were deemed strong and worth buying.

This theory was easy to justify. If a currency was suspect, you sold it as soon as you got it: you did not hold it or lend it. Therefore, there were few lenders. Nor did you buy it when you needed it: you tried to borrow it and hoped to buy it later, after it had devalued. Thus, few lenders, many borrowers, high rates of interest.

The opposite applied to good or hard currencies. Nobody is fool enough to delay buying what is thought likely to appreciate soon. Nor does anyone sell now what may fetch a higher price tomorrow. Therefore there are many holders of such a currency who want to lend, but few borrowers. Thus, many lenders, few borrowers, low rates of interest.

This theory was turned on its head a few years ago. Monetarist economics have recognized the importance of relating money supply to productivity. Cheap credit and easy credit are the parents of inflation.

This is not the place to discuss and evaluate how precisely true these doctrines are. It is, however, necessary to note that high interest rates at a time of strong inflationary tendencies have become symbols of governmental virtue. This was the great economic innovation of the late seventies and resulted, briefly one may hope, in the oversimplified view that rates of interest are the only valid indicators of future movements in exchange rates.

This view had two separate justifications.

1. Governments must use interest rates to control the money supply and therefore the rate of inflation. The higher the rates of interest, the more heroic and virtuous the government. This is an alarming oversimplification of proper governmental action, as we now tend to see.
2. High interest rates will attract money from abroad and low interest rates will drive it out again. This is not true: changes in exchange rates are much more important than even the greatest interest rate differentials between major currencies.

I believe that all that is certain is the following:

(a) as long as the interest rate–exchange rate relationship is believed in blindly by the majority (as probably it was for much of 1980 and 1981) we are prone to get a self-fulfilling prophecy, and

(b) there are of course always individual speculators who at any particular threshold (change in the rate of interest) will think that the extra return on money now justifies the exchange risk and will move some funds out of one currency and into another. This does not mean that the interest rate alone has caused them to take this decision.

Trade figures and money flows as major influences

There was a time when the published trade figures were eagerly awaited. Good or bad figures showing a surplus or a deficit on visible trade were debated in advance, discounted by the market prophets, marvelled at upon publication, dissected, disputed and discussed. Changes for the better or for the worse could move exchange rates and even precipitate crises. Invisibles were less easily understood and presented as an excellent argument to foster or counter speculation. Exact borrowings and loan repayments by government were frequently unclear.

The balance of trade and changes in the balance of trade are without doubt of great importance in assessing a country's ability to keep to the present rate of exchange. The difficulty lies in doing so with a reasonable degree of accuracy.

The exchange rate expresses the balance between demand and supply of the national currency in the international currency markets. Exports and imports must balance or the exchange rate will move: it is a price like any other.

The trade figures alone are, however, no valid indicator. How important are inward and outward investment? How big are short-term money flows inward or outward, and how likely are they to change? What credit is available, and how much has been and how much will be taken? Are existing loans due to be repaid, will they be repaid on time or ahead of time or will they be recycled? Are some trade terms affected by normal or by unusual seasonal factors? Have developments in money markets or changes in exchange control or in government insurance schemes here or abroad altered the size of commercial credit taken or given?

When all this is known, we can begin to cull useful exchange rate information from the published figures concerning the balance of payments.

Politics and fashion in a free market

Only a fool would seek to obtain all his indications from one area alone. Notwithstanding this, most traders in any market develop over the years an inclination to look to one or two areas for the indicators they find decisive. Their conclusion is personal and the defence of it should not be too dogmatic.

Economic policy holds the key to political success in the world of today. The level of the exchange rate is of paramount importance to the economic and social policy of any government. This is so whether the government admits it or not. It is so whether the government believes in trying to put the exchange rate where it wants it or in accepting the level at which the forces of the free market have placed it.

It follows that political decisions or the absence of them can and often do override all the economic indicators. The decisions of governments have considerable influence upon exchange rates, even though their power in this field is far from absolute. A good dealer will try to understand politics and the politicians.

There is only one force which is stronger than the government in a free market. This is the sentiment of the operators in the market. In the case of foreign exchange these operators are bank dealers, company treasurers, speculators and central bankers, all of them exercising an influence on the price of currencies by what they say or don't say and by what they do or don't do.

Because they are a part of a market they are inclined to share moods and feelings and fears and prejudices. They are subject to collective emotions which are best described as fashions. For many years the dollar was unassailable. Then the mark was in favour and then the yen. The dollar recovered and even the unspeakable pound has received some remarkable fan mail since becoming a petrocurrency. With the benefit of hindsight most of these moods were overdone and resulted in swings beyond those which were economically justified.

Fashion is the ultimate motive in a market where keeping up with the Joneses is often both easiest intellectually and most profitable commercially.

Summary

Foreign exchange problems are bewildering and fascinating. Their successful solution is nowadays economically vital to most firms. Before the stability of Bretton Woods was replaced by the uncertainties and complexities of floating exchange rates this was true only for the few.

A combination of factual knowledge and feel for the market, of economic theories and intuitive responses can lead to the right answers. The way to obtain these and to mix them in their proper proportions is through the growing discipline of risk evaluation and exposure control.

Companies engaged in any international activity must know the size of their exposure, currency by currency and period by period. They must update it frequently. They must study the likelihood of adverse movements in rates and the proportion of their business which such movements would affect. They need to obtain economic and political information, both detailed and sophisticated. They need to listen to their bankers and their consultants. Above all else, they must have an in-house policy on foreign exchange, developed and applied by a team of managers with relevant knowledge and experience.

FURTHER READING

(Compiled by Weisweiller Adfos, March 1984)

General reading

Foreign Exchange Markets, H. Riehl & R. M. Rodriguez (McGraw-Hill 1977).
Money Hard and Soft, Brendan Brown (Macmillan 1978).
Devisen: Werkzeug des Welthandels, Rudi Weisweiller (Prugg Verlag Vienna 1978).
'The Exchange Rate as an Instrument of Policy', Otmar Emminger (*Lloyds Bank Review* July 1979).
Money and Exchange Dealing in International Banking, Nigel R. L. Hudson (Macmillan 1979).
Foreign Exchange Today (revised edition), Raymond G. F. Coninx (Woodhead-Faulkner 1980).
A Guide for Using the Foreign Exchange Market, T. Walker (John Wiley 1981).
Basic Handbook of Foreign Exchange, Claude Tygier (Euromoney 1983).

Foreign exchange language

A Dictionary of International Finance, Julian Walmsley (Macmillan 1979).

The London market

The London Foreign Exchange Market (Forex Association London 1980).
Foreign Exchange Dealer's Handbook, Raymond G. F. Coninx (Woodhead-Faulkner 1982).
The Management and Regulation of Banks, John Cooper (Macmillan 1983).

Eurodollars

The Economics of the Eurocurrency System, G. W. McKenzie (Macmillan 1976).
The Euromarkets and International Financial Policies, D. F. Lomax & P. T. G. Gutmann (Macmillan 1981).

For the company treasurer

Foreign Exchange Risk, A. R. Prindl (John Wiley 1976).

Foreign Exchange and the Corporate Treasurer, John Heywood (A. & C. Black 1978).
Exchange Risk & Corporate International Finance, Robert Z. Aliber (John Wiley 1978).
Management of Foreign Exchange Risk, L. L. Jacque (Lexington 1978).
Foreign Exchange Management and the Multinational Corporation, A. M. George (Praeger 1978).
Corporate Currency Risk, J. A. Donaldson (Financial Times Business Publications 1980).
'Currency Risk', edited by Boris Antl (*Euromoney* 1980).
'The Management of Foreign Exchange Risk', edited by Richard Ensor & Boris Antl (*Euromoney* 1981).
Currency Risk Management, P. H. A. Kenyon (John Wiley 1981).
Foreign Exchange Management, T. W. McRae & D. P. Walker (Prentice Hall 1981).
Currency Management, Richard Lassen (Woodhead-Faulkner 1982).
A Guide for Using the Foreign Exchange Market, T. Walker (John Wiley 1981).
Guidelines on Foreign Exchange, S. Bell and B. Kettell (Graham & Trotman 1983).
Medium Term Exchange Rate Guidelines for Business Planning, Bill Robinson (Gower 1983).

Financial Futures

An Introduction to Financial Futures (Butler Till 1982).
Financial Futures (Arthur Andersen 1982).

The International Monetary Market (27 Throgmorton Street, London EC2) and the London International Financial Futures Exchange (Royal Exchange, London EC3) also publish informative brochures.

Currency Options

Understanding Foreign Currency Options (Philadelphia Stock Exchange 1983).

INDEX

Asian dollars, definition of, 117
automatic recycling, definition of, 101

balance of payments, 2, 4, 74, 79, 88, 124
   effect of public relations on, 112–113
   imbalance in, 103–104, 108, 109–111, 111–114
   and inflation, 113–114
   and reserves, 106, 111
Bank for International Settlements, 48, 101, 111
Bank of England, and exchange control, 87–88, 89
banks,
   foreign exchange departments of, 30–32
   as intermediaries, 8–15
basket currencies, 56–57
   definition of, 56
Basle agreements, 59, 81–82
Bretton Woods Conference, 6, 48–57, 83, 139
   effects of, 52–53
   philosophy of, 52
brokers,
   Eurocurrency, 123
   role of, 10–13
brokers' markets, 12

capital movements, 91–95
central rate, *see* parity
convertibility,
   advantages of, 90
   and currency freedom, 84–85
   definition of, 84
covered arbitrage, 38–40
   see also interest arbitrage
crawling peg system, 54–55
cross deals, definition of, 19
cross rates, definition of, 18–19
currency area, 58, 59
   see also sterling area

currency crises, 103–116
   avoidance of, 107–109
   causes of, 104–107
   prevention of, 114–115
currency developments, theories of forecasting, 134–139
currency freedom, 84–89
currency invoicing, 27–30
   and exports, 28
   and imports, 28–29
currency options, 35–36
currency reserves, 82, 105–107, 107–109, 109–111

dealers,
   and brokers, 10, 11, 12
   and deposit brokers, 12–13
   as spectators, 99–100
dealing,
   between centres, 14–15
   systems, 8–15
deflation, 63, 107, 114
delivery date, *see* value date
demonetization, 80, 82
   practice of, 72–74
   theory of, 72
deposit broker, 12–13
devaluation, 42, 44, 63, 82, 107, 115, 135
   and crawling peg system, 54
   and interest arbitrage, 42, 44
direct dealing, 14
direct investment, 122
discount, 17–18
   definition of, 18
Dollar Certificates of Deposit, 123
dollar premium, 91
dual currency system, 91–93

Emminger, Dr Otmar, 78
Eurobond market, development of, 123

Index   143

Eurocurrencies, 119–120
  see also Eurodollars
Eurocurrency borrowing, risks of, 127–129
Eurocurrency brokers, 123
Eurocurrency markets,
  dangers of, 125–127
  and deposit brokers, 12
  development of, 121–123
  future of, 123–125
Eurodollar market, 119, 121–123
  see also Eurocurrency markets
Eurodollars, 117–129
  definition of, 117
  origins of, 118–119
European Currency Unit (ECU), 57, 117
European Monetary Co-operation Fund, 66
European Monetary System (EMS), 24, 55, 57, 66, 101
  advantages and disadvantages of, 66–67
  development of, 66
exchange control, 22, 61, 114
  definition of, 85
  future of, 87–90
  justification for, 85–87
  role of Bank of England in, 87–88, 89
  suspension of, 61
Exchange Control Act 1947, 58, 87
exchange control area, 59–61
  see also sterling area
exchange rate, 2–4, 37–39, 41, 43
  definition of, 2
  forecasting of, 130–133, 138–139
  see also fashions, floating exchange rate, politics
exchange risks, and interest arbitrage, 38, 39, 41, 42, 44–45

fashions, effect on exchange rate, 139
Federal Reserve Bank, 123
financial futures, 34–35
fixed-date forward contracts, 26–27
fixing, *see* foreign exchange bourse
floating exchange rate, 92, 99
  change to, 53–54
foreign exchange, basic principles of, 1–5
foreign exchange bourse, 13–14
foreign exchange departments, *see* banks

foreign exchange market, 2, 5–7
  and money markets, 45–46
  workings of, 8–21
Forex Club, *see* International Foreign Exchange Club
forward cover, 40, 43, 44, 45, 46, 89
  advantages and disadvantages of, 22–25
  guidelines to, 25–26
forward deals, definition of, 17
forward rates, meaning and significance of, 43–44

gold, monetary, 69–76
  alternatives to as reserve unit, 75–76
  and paper money, 74–75
  price rises of, 69–70
  see also demonetization, speculation
gold market,
  price rises of, 73–74
  two-tier system of, 70, 72
  uses of, 70–71
Gold Pool, 72
  history of, 70–71
  improvement of, 73–74
gold reserves, 70, 73–74, 75
gold standard, 74–75

hard currencies, 30, 136
hedging, definition of, 34
hot money, 5, 38, 41–43

inflation, 93, 110, 113, 114
  definition of, 109
  rates of as indicators, 135
interest arbitrage, 37–47
  and business transactions, 44–45
  covered, 38–40
  definition of, 6
  practice versus theory of, 40–41
  theory of, 37–38
  see also exchange risks, interest rates
interest rates,
  and exchange rate, 135–137
  and interest arbitrage, 37, 38, 39, 40, 41, 42, 43, 44, 50
International Foreign Exchange Club, 13, 21
International Monetary Fund (IMF), 6, 53, 72, 73, 74, 82, 101, 111, 115
  setting up of, 48–49
  and Special Drawing Rights, 78, 79, 83
  Statutes of, 53, 55, 81, 89, 91

144   Index

intervention by central banks, 6–7, 43
   in forward market, 50–51
   in spot market, 51–52
intervention points, 6, 49–50, 51, 95
   and crawling peg system, 54
   criticism of, 54
investment currency, 91, 93–95
investment currency pool, definition of, 93
investment currency premium, 94–95
investment dollar pool, definition of, 93
   see also investment currency pool
investment dollars, 91, 93, 94
   see also investment currency
invoicing, *see* currency invoicing

lags, definition of, 97
language of foreign exchange, 4
   misunderstandings in, 20–21
   problem of, 16
   terms of, 17–20
leads, definition of, 97
Letters of Intent, 48
liquidity, *see* world liquidity
London Foreign Exchange Market, 7, 10

managed floating, 54
middle rate, definition of, 81
monetary gold, *see* gold
money flows, 91
   influence on exchange rate, 137–138
money markets, 5
   and foreign exchange markets, 45–46
Morse Committee of the Group of Twenty, 55
Multinational Exchange Rate Model, 56

numeraire, 56
   definition of, 81

one-tier system, 72
   see also Gold Pool
option contracts:
   currency options, 35–36
   time options, 26–27
ordinary spot, *see* spot

paper gold, *see* Special Drawing Rights
par value, *see* parity
parities,
   fixed, 53, 54, 55, 99
   floating, 53, 55
parity, 49, 52, 66, 67, 135
   definition of, 81
politics, effect on exchange rate, 138–139
portfolio investment, 91
   definition of, 89
premium, 17–18
   definition of, 18
premium dollars, 91
   see also investment dollars, investment currency
Purchasing Power Parity Theory of Money, 135

quotations, 32–34

reserve currency, 64
   role of European currencies as, 68
   use of national currencies as, 61
reserves, 77–78
   definition of, 77
   see also currency reserves, gold reserves
revaluation, 63, 115, 135

short-term borrowing, and balance of payments, 111–112
Smithsonian Settlement, 53, 56
snake, 66
   definition of, 62
   development of, 64–65
snake in the tunnel, 65
   definition of, 62
sovereign risks, 126
Special Drawing Rights, 56, 58, 69–70, 72, 74, 75, 77–83, 110, 117
   definition of, 79
   as numeraire, 81
   use of, 79–80
   as world currency, 81–83
speculation, 96–102, 105
   definition of, 6
   and gold, 70, 71, 73, 76
   see also speculators
speculators, 50, 137
   and governments, 101–102
   morality of, 98
   and public relations, 112–113
   role of, 99–101
   types of, 96–97

spot,
  cover, 22–25, 45
  definition of, 17
  exchange rate, 37, 39, 43
  ordinary, 17, 18
sterling area, 58–61, 82
  definition of, 58
swaps, 13, 74, 111
  advantages and disadvantages of, 26–27
  definition of, 19–20

time options, 26–27
trade figures, influence on exchange rate, 137–138

trade-weighted index, definition of, 56
Treasury Bills, 34
Treaty of Rome, 62, 91
tunnel, *see* snake in the tunnel
two-tier system, 70, 72
  see also gold market

US Federal Reserve System, 118

value date, definition of, 17

Werner Plan, 62–64
world liquidity,
  future of, 80–81
  shortage of, 78, 79
worm, definition of, 64, 65